Belgium's Magnificent Seven

Arthur Haulot,
General Commissioner
for Tourism.

For several years now the National Tourist Office has tried to make both the Belgian and foreign public more aware of the many and varied treasures our country has to offer the tourist. With this aim we have launched a number of campaigns — on Gallo-Roman relics (1959), our shells (1961), our windmills (1962), museums (1969), castles (1971 and 1972), abbeys and convents (1973), folklore (1974), cathedrals and town halls (1975), historic parks and gardens (1976), and the prestige of Rubens and the Belgian painters (1977).

Our ambition was to crown this series of spectacular campaigns in 1978 with the theme « Seven Wonders of Belgium ». Not that there are only seven masterpieces in Belgium, but we believed that as a result of promoting the seven the whole marvellous spectrum of art, architecture, history and man's creative spirit would be revealed. The choice was easy. Certain works were firmly fixed in the minds of eminent connoisseurs and historians.

But we wanted something more, and better, than a simple publicity campaign. Having said many times how much we believe in the necessity and the virtue of correctly informing the public, we wanted the Seven Wonders to be the starting point of a new cultural arousing.

Our meeting with Professor d'Haenens, who had just completed a documentary montage on the prestigious history of the University of Louvain, decided the method. So each chosen work is now presented to the public as a spectacle of great historic, scientific and technical value which puts fundamental understanding within the range of everyone. To give the chance to see is certainly good, but to help to learn is in our opinion even better. The union of technique and creative enthusiasm allows this experiment to be made for the first time on a nationwide basis.

Running parallel to our efforts are those of a well-established Belgian publisher, adding to our enterprise the value of the written word and the subtle image. In wishing the publisher success, we are thinking mostly of the public, a public which has always shown itself prepared for any new adventure when properly approached.

Belgium's Magnificent Seven

Elsevier

This book was conceived and produced in close collaboration
between *Editions Elsevier*
and *Professor Albert d'Haenens*
of the Catholic University of Louvain,
and with the cooperation of *M. De Somer, P. Orban, G. Lemaire, G. Zélis, C. Pinson, M. Stessel, J-P. Nandrin, Th. Symons*
of the Centre for Research into Communication in History,
and of *M.R. Lapière, R. Didier, Ch. Malaise, E. Dhanens, D. Hollanders, R. Ph. Roberts-Jones, J. Van Ackere,* art historians

The publishers also wish to acknowledge the participation of the following :

Ian Gretton, translation
Michel Olyff, design, lay-out and covers
Jean-Jacques Rousseau, drawings
Remy Magermans, photogravure
Petrus van Roemburg and *Bernard Fasbender*, technical coordination
Geneviève Dupont and *Guido Peeters*, general coordination

The author and publishers express their gratitude to all museum curators, owners and keepers of works of art who have allowed the works in their possession to be reproduced here.

© 1978 Elsevier Séquoia, Brussels.
ISBN : 2-8003-0309-3
D/1978/0027/069

Printed in Belgium
by *Graphing*, Jumet.

Foreword

Made in metal, in painted wood or on canvas, here are seven works representing the essential aspect of Belgium's cultural heritage, which in its precious works bears witness to our ancestors' preoccupations. They constitute a genuine anthology of the know-how, sensitivity, aims and hopes of our forefathers — those to whom we owe our existence. And because they describe to us what was regarded as important and beautiful by them, they make up a unique part of our material, cultural and spiritual heritage. Those who commissioned works of art were not always the princes of the world. But they had wealth and power and they used their temporal and social influence to open the door to posterity, the only approach to the unattainable eternity. For them works of art were the most promising and most durable investments.

They also dictated to the artists the materials they believed would be most suitable. In the 12th and 13th centuries in Liège, Tournai and Oignies there was no shortage of precious metals and their exchange value was still symbolic. These clerks and citizens felt their use could ideally serve the dual goal they sought — the reflection of how highly they thought of the artists they judged worthy of working with such materials, and the harmonisation of the outstanding qualities of the donors, witness of their material and social success, with those of the Church and those represented on earth by the Church. The result dazzles our senses and our spirit, be it a baptismal font, a shrine, a chalice, an evangeliary or another form of reliquary.

In the 15th century in Bruges and Ghent, in the Brussels and Antwerp of the 16th and 17th centuries, precious metals were beginning to be much used for non-sacred purposes, and they were replaced by pictoral representations which, freed from Byzantine lines, won a freedom of expression which made them ideal for those who commissioned new works. They would commission a painted shrine, a reredos and a monumental tryptich. To display their wealth and culture they would buy non-sacred works.

These are the origins of the metal creations of the Meuse and Rhine valleys, still worked today by the metallurgical industry, and of the pictoral creations dear to the dynamic traders.

The fact that six of these objects had a religious function is no coincidence. At that time the sacred was essential and religion played a prominent part in everyday life. It was practised with solemn celebrations requiring lofty decor, such as baptism, a perfect example of the initiation and introduction into the Christian community, and communal Eucharists which strengthened the links between various groups. There was also the veneration of relics which exalted the saints whose remains were kept in the reliquaries and gleaming shrines. Commissioning fonts, reliquaries and altar-screens was the best way to take part in the principal liturgical actions. No doubt it was also an investment in eternity.

The men who created these works are often unknown, and when we do know their names we know little about their lives, with the exception of Rubens and possibly Brueghel. The personalities of these men cannot be summed up in a few biographical details. We often know nothing more than the place and approximate date of their birth, or where they stayed during a journey or lived at one stage in their careers. These outstanding artists seem to have raised little interest among their contemporaries who wrote what was to enter posterity. In the Middle Ages one tended to remember those who commissioned the works rather than those who created them, as if it were considered more important to provoke an event than to take part in it. Obscure or otherwise, the people who created these works show a striking mastery of their craft. They perfected not only one technique but several. Renier of Huy, for example, was an epigraphist, a sculptor and a founder. Hugo d'Oignies was an imitator, a miniaturist, a designer and a gold and silversmith. As for Brueghel, he can be considered as much a painter as a philosopher, a sociologist and an artist.

This artistic and intellectual diversification provides a sharp contrast with present-day specialisation. Our creators are humanists in all senses of the word.

Because they were such complete masters of their technique their expression has perfect legibility and transparency. They expressed themselves several centuries ago, but today they still adress us with great strength. They speak the everlasting language of those who find the time and the way to express man and his world. Like all genuine creations, theirs are timeless and of all times.

These seven objects also tell us about the people for whom they were intended, their problems and their perennial fears, the answers the clergy gave them — the story of the crucial moments of their redemption, of those who were their intermediaries in Heaven, of the saints. In fact, the story of the people of God on their way to salvation, the story of man and his quest for Heaven.

On the sides of the Liège fonts men with harmonious, lissom forms talk with the Prophets and the Son of God. Here in the still rigid plasticity of the early 12th century are serenity, balance and perfection. All over the Notre Dame reliquary are men and women with a nobility and a majesty which recall Chartres, Rheims and Paris, demonstrating classical perfection at the dawn of the Gothic era. On the metal binding of the Oignies evangeliary the vegetal friezes are brought to life by hunters and game, the Crucifixion and the Divine Majesty. Hugo has achieved in metal all the finesse and delicacy of manuscript illumination.

The Mystic Lamb, an « enormous miniature » according to Paul Claudel, is an exceptional and audacious project which puts the doctrine of the Redemption into images. There is a realism in which the painter dares to paint everything, a humanism which equates man with his God.

On the oak panels of a Gothic reliquary Hans Memling tells the story of Ursula in luminous, urban chapters.

A legend thus far only known through writing and story-telling is recounted in marvellous images. Pieter Brueghel introduces a break from tradition. Man is sent back to live with himself and his daily life. He who wants to escape finds only unhappiness. His wings are too fragile and he creshes into the waves.

The Descent from the Cross was a real challenge to painters, but Rubens, the complete master of the Baroque, made an intense act of faith of this triumph of colour, form and design.

Seven objects which must be discovered and analysed so that they may be understood and admired. As with many others for which they act almost as spokesmen, they bear witness to the relationship between matter and spirit, between technical mastery and artistic creation, between labour and art.

Professor Albert d'Haenens

Baptismal Fonts

or the Masterpiece of Roman Art

Renier of Huy

Liège

Church of Saint Barthélemy

In the 11th and 12th centuries
the Mosan region
abounded in metalworkers
and craftsmen ; miners, blacksmiths,
gold and silversmiths of quality,
whose specialised trades
required them to serve long
apprenticeships
and master an astonishing number
of skills and techniques.

The subsoil was rich in iron and zinc ores and the region was a natural centre for metallurgical production. The river provided an inexpensive means of transport to and from the North Sea and England, even to the Mediterranean via Champagne and the Rhone.

On the forested banks of the Meuse, with their potential for metal production, grew up industrial towns, resting places for boats and carts, places where goods and ideas were exchanged.

**Liège :
a prestigious
12th century centre**

Of all the Mosan towns Liège had become the most prestigious by the beginning of the 12th century. Daughter of the Meuse and of the Church, it was at the same time capital, diocesan centre and cultural centre. The builder, Notger, had planned it a hundred years earlier. He had surrounded it with « a network of moats and a girdle of stone » (Jean Lejeune). The prince who lived there as the centre of his principality was a friend and devoted representative of the Emperor.

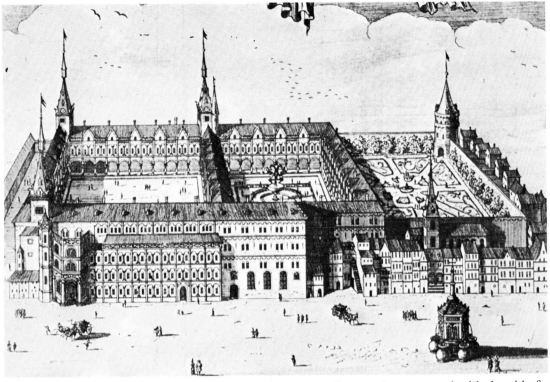

Bishop and head of the diocese, he governed with the aid of knowledgeable clerks who knew both Athens and Byzantium. His schools were particularly famous, and the cream of the western world was educated there.

Ever since the seventh century an ecclesiastical group had lived in parts of the bishop's palace and around the market. It was common in the Europe of the Middle Ages for the various religious services to take place in a number of places and not, as today, in a single sanctuary.

There was the Church of Saint Lambert, built on the site where the saint was martyred and run by a community of clerks who advised the bishop. The Church of Saint Peter, built by Saint Hubert and dedicated to the funereal cult. The primitive parish church of Notre-Dame-aux-Fonts, which alone had the right to conduct baptisms.

Mould of the counter-seal of the chapter-house of Liège (1243), one of the rare representations of Notre-Dame-aux-Fonts.

Hellin : the originator

It is possible that the masterpiece of Renier of Huy originated from an argument over precedence between Notre-Dame-aux-Fonts, which belonged to the chapter-house of the cathedral, and the Church of Saint Adalbert, which was under the jurisdiction of the canons of Saint John the Evangelist.

The dispute was over the right to conduct baptisms, which Saint Adalbert claimed to have been given by Notger and which it exercised in the very heart of the town - the Isle - to the detriment of Notre-Dame-aux-Fonts.

Twice, in 1101 and 1107, the question was raised at the episcopal synod by the abbot of Notre-Dame who wanted his church to keep the monopoly on baptisms. On both occasions his complaint was rejected.

Hellin, who became abbot of Notre-Dame shortly after 1107, installed a baptismal font so striking that it could not fail to attract both admirers and candidates for baptism. He had been educated at Fosses and then, most likely, at the monastery of Gembloux. He became canon at Saint Bartholomew's in Liège, then abbot of the Church of Notre-Dame-aux-Fonts.

A splendid ivory, currently housed in the Curtius Museum. Bishop Notger, kneeling before the chapel of Saint Adalbert, holds a scroll which is reputed to contain the text granting permission for baptisms to be held in the chapel.

The baptismal bowl is cylindrical, 60 cm in height and 80 cm in diameter. The characters illustrated vary in height from 29 to 38 cm, the upper and lower mouldings are 6 and 6.5 cm respectively. The oxen which support the work vary in height from 18 to 20 cm, and in length from 21 to 25 cm. Opening out slightly towards the top, the fonts were completed by a cover which disappeared during the French Revolution. It depicted the Prophets and the Apostles, a link between the Old and New Testaments.

Renier : the craftsman

Hellin approached Renier of Huy, without doubt the most accomplished craftsman in metal of his time in the Mosan region.

However, we know little about the Hutois craftsman's work. Chroniclers of the Middle Ages tend to recall those who commissioned the most prestigious works, but not the craftsmen who made them. The author of the *Chronique liégeoise of 1402* is the first to mention that the fonts were the work of Renier, gold and silversmith of Huy. Among his principal sources is a document dating from Renier's time, a charter granted in 1125 by Bishop Alberon II (1123-1128) to the Church of Notre Dame in Huy in which one *Reinerus aurifaber* is mentioned among the lay worshippers. Renier died around 1150, on December 4 according to the Huy abbey records of Neufmoustier. To Renier abbot Hellin described the scenes he wished to have depicted on the fonts' surrounds. He had found them in the Old Testament, in the Gospels, the Acts of the Apostles and in the writings of Saint Augustine.

Renier first built a model which he used as his guide throughout the making of the font.

With the aid of a team of specialised assistants, the craftsman builds a core from clay mixed with straw and dung. This he covers with a layer of wax, gently heated and at a constant thickness, and in the wax he models his characters, his bas-relief sculptures and the inscriptions.

After this comes the mould. The wax core is coated with several thin layers of clay with special care taken over the escape ducts for the wax and gases, and after each layer it is left out in the sun to dry. Then it is heated to remove the melted-dow wax.

It is then placed upside down on a bed of coal, carefully surrounded by a wall of unmortared reflective bricks. The coal is lit and maintained at a constant temperature until the mould is white hot.

This is followed by the casting. The team thoroughly washes down the clay with water to avoid shrinkage when the metal solidifies, and the mould is placed in a pit. The vats of brass (an alloy of copper, tin and calamine) are heated and the liquid poured into where the wax had been.

Eventually the mould is lifted from the pit and the clay and the core removed. All that remains is for the metalsmith to add his final touches.

The function of the font

According to the Christian doctrine, men are born with the original sin which prevents them from entering the kingdom of God.

Baptismal water, the source of life, washes away this sin and regenerates the baptised.

In early Christian times adults were baptised together in groups. Men and women wishing to become members of the Christian community were immersed in a specially built pool in the baptistery. But the sacrement became more and more personalised, and the pool was gradually replaced by the baptismal font. New-born babies were baptised from the height of the Middle Ages. Baptismal water, blessed on the eve of Easter or Whitsuntide and preserved in the font, was poured over the head of the child.

**The originality
of Renier's creation**

The baptismal fonts of Saint Bartholomew's have no known predecessors. In the diocese of Liège stone baptismal bowls predominated, and those which have survived from the 11th and 12th centuries reveal a simple art with an architectonic decor of plants or animals.

Man rarely appeared, and when he did, he was so roughly represented that no real comparison between the examples which remain - such as the fonts of Furnaux - and those of Renier of Huy is possible. For a century his style was to have a profound influence on the gold and silversmiths of the Mosan region.

But Renier's fonts were never copied, they remained alone in their perfection. A comparison between the brass baptismal bowl in the Church of Saint-Germain at Tienen, probably a Brabant work dating from 1149, says a great deal on this subject. There was a copy which was carved in stone by a 12th century Moselle sculptor who fashioned the baptismal fonts in the old chapel of the Château of Mousson. But it is an imitation which achieves neither the classical beauty of Renier's creation nor the beliefs on which it was based.

**A combination
of Christian belief
and ancient beauty**

Historians agree that the baptismal fonts of Saint
Bartholomew's represent a mixture of the arts of Greece,
Rome and Byzantium, all perfectly worked together by an
artist who has achieved classical beauty. The characters
sculpted in high relief around the base of the bowl bring
Ancient Greece to mind. At the same time, the baptismal
frieze and the uneven ground with its rows of trees are
reminiscent of the illusionist art of Pergamos and Alexandria.
One of the leading experts on the work, Marcel Laurent, has
tried to pin down one of the sources of Renier's inspiration.
To him the general form of the bowl is reminiscent of the
putealia, those circular curbs with which the Romans
surrounded their wells, as well as places struck by lightning,
which they believed to be sacred.
But Renier had other sources of inspiration which recalled
earlier times. The Mosan soil is rich in those little
Gallo-Roman bronzes whose moulding must have fascinated
craftsmen of the era ; the works of the 11th century Mosan
ivory-workers who, influenced by the ivory-workers of Metz
and the Remois miniaturists of the Carolingian period,
perpetuated the memory of Greek naturalism. But the
influence of ancient art appears above all in the general order
of the work, in the purity of the moulding of the characters,
in the value which the craftsman knew to give to the open
spaces.
The Byzantine influence shows itself in the details of the
imagery, particularly in the baptism of Christ. The distinct
way of representing the river Jordan, for example, or the
hands of the angels, veiled by gauze as a mark of respect.
This influence is not exclusive to the baptismal fonts of Saint-
Bartholomew's. Ever since the Carolingian era Western
Europe had regularly received Byzantine works of art,
materials, gold and silver objects, imported relics, all of
which fired the creative imagination of artists.
Renier was no exception. But he assimilated the various
influences with a supreme skill and transcended them with a
genius which is obvious to men of all eras.

A clear and simple composition

The form of the fonts is that of a cylindrical bowl, gradually opening out towards the top and hemmed at the base and the top by a moulded projection. These bear inscriptions explaining and complementing the legends which accompany each scene around the base.

The uneven floor, covered with a thin layer of brass, along with the two rims, creates a ternary rhythm. It modifies the nature of the smooth base to which it is set perpendicularly, the opaque screen producing an ethereal effect.

The trees, generally regarded to be palms and oaks, complete the illusion. They are not merely decorative. Their uneven trunks, solidly joined to the base, then suddenly moving away from it, contribute to the overall effect of space. They are also useful in understanding the work in that they separate the scenes without disuniting them.

Five baptismal scenes

There are about 20 high relief characters making up the scenes, and all are focussed upon a central theme, the baptism of Christ by John the Baptist. Waist-deep in the water, Christ holds up His right hand in blessing. The raised thumb, index and forefinger evoke the Holy Trinity. Above the head of Christ the sky opens, and the images of the Father and the Holy Ghost appear, their wings casting light on Him and sanctifying the baptism which is taking place.

John the Baptist places his right hand on the head of Jesus, at the same time holding up the hem of his rough hide garment, the mark of the hermits of the Palestinian desert. John's face bears a serenely grave expression. Christ, the spiritual centre of the piece, has a juvenile and delicate allure. The inscriptions engraved on the base are all directed towards Him. First, the words of the Father : « This is my beloved Son, in whom I am well pleased » (Matthew, 3, 17). Then the reply of John the Baptist to Christ, who has asked to be baptised in the same way as all the humble citizens of Jerusalem and the neighbouring towns who come to John : « I have need to be baptised of thee, and comest thou to me ? » (Matthew, 3, 14).

Thus begins the public life of Christ, an historic moment described by a theologian who chose the images the craftsman was to depict on the font. There is no communication between the principal characters in the central scene. Christ is already removed from the material world, seeking the infinite. Instead, one's attention is drawn to the human confrontation in the first two episodes of the iconographical cycle. They foreshadow the baptism of Christ and depict the Baptist in his evangelical mission.

Here, according to Luke (3, 1-18), John the Baptist preaches repentance to the crowd. They ask him : « What shall we do ? » To the publicans, Herod's tax collectors, he answers : « Exact no more than that which is appointed you ». To the soldiers : « Do violence to no man, neither accuse any falsely ; and be content with your wages ». The evident diversity of sentiments provoked by John the Baptist's sermon is marvellously illustrated by Renier. The prophet has clearly shaken the first two members of the group : the publican in the foreground, wearing medieval clothes, and the soldier, in his helmet and suit of chain mail and carrying a sword like those of the knights of the 12th century. But are they convinced ? The soldier nervously raises a finger, wishing to know more. The reactions of the two other listeners, partly hidden by their companions, seem clearer. The young, fresh-faced man, his head covered by a cap, is undoubtedly touched by the grace. His bright face is fixed upon the speaker, his lips bear a smile. The fourth man is also smiling. Sceptical, he assesses at a glance the slim figure

of the prophet standing before him. The problem of arranging the group has been solved skilfully. John the Baptist appears in the foreground, his tall figure pushing his audience into the background, the depth of which is accentuated by the superposition of the characters.

The baptism of the neophytes is a logical successor to the previous scene. John the Baptist appears much as we have seen him in earlier groups, but this time he is naked. His body is that of a hermit with prominent ribs, contrasting sharply with the Hellenic plasticity of the sleek naked bodies of the two young men he is baptising. Above their stooping forms the inscription explains the scene and gives it its theological value : « I indeed baptise you with water, but he that cometh after me is mightier than I » (Matthew, 3, 11 ; Mark, 1, 7). The personalities of the two men on the banks of the Jordan are less clearly established. According to most experts they are recent candidates for baptism. According to J. Puraye they are disciples of the Baptist who will leave him to follow Christ : « Again the next day after John stood, and two of his disciples ; and looking upon Jesus as he walked, he saith, Behold the Lamb of God ! And the two disciples heard him speak, and they followed Jesus » (John 1, 35-37). Indeed, on closer inspection, the second character seems to be turning back. Eventually, he leaves the banks of the river, his steps - examine the position of his feet - guiding him resolutely away. Etched into the metal by the skill of the craftsman, his body, or what one can see of it beneath the flowing lines of his tunic, is one of the most expressive on the baptismal fonts.

Completing the perimeter of the bowl are two scenes which
succeed the baptism of Christ : the baptism of the centurion
Cornelius and that of Craton the Philosopher. A Roman and a
Greek, since the divine grace is universal and « the Holy
Ghost descends upon all who listen to the word ».

This is engraved in the brass, the lesson to be learned from
the story of Cornelius, leader of a group of a hundred
legionaires belonging to the Italian cohort of Caesarea,
whose conversion and baptism are described in the Acts of
the Apostles (10, 1-48). Here it is Saint Peter who officiates.
His reluctance to baptise a Gentile was overcome by a
miraculous intervention, described in the text of the scroll
which he holds in his left hand : « What was I, that I could
withstand God ? » (Acts, 11, 17).

The inscriptions on the adjoining scene are less explicit. The
story of Craton, a philosopher of Ephesus who was converted

These two examples of baptism by immersion, panels from the same diptych, symbolise the universality and the evangelical vigour of a Christianity into which were accepted both Cornelius and Craton, the imperial power and the Greek influence.

by John the Evangelist, is not related in the Bible other than by apocryphal reference. In addition, the commissioner of the work exerted a sort of censorship, and all we see here are the names of the two principal characters and the words *Dextera Dei* in capitals.

A universe of symbolism

Renier's work represents a wealth of symbols. The oxen, for example (there are now only ten of them representing the Apostles) : « In the twelve oxen are represented the figures of the shepherds, simultaneously prescribing the grace of the apostolic life and the joy with which this river delights the holy town and purifies its citizens ». (Leonine lines of the lower edges of the bowl.) Their presence evokes the sea of brass which King Solomon ordered from the brassworker Hiram for the temple of Jehovah : « And he made a molten sea, ten cubits from one brim to the other ; it was round all about, and its height was five cubits... It stood upon twelve oxen, three looking toward the north, and three looking toward the west, and three looking toward the south, and three looking toward the east : and the sea was set above upon them, and all their hinder parts were inward » (1 Kings, 7, 23-26).

The establishment of precise links between the facts of the Old and New Testaments — typological symbolism — was popular with the Liège theologians of the period. One of the most illustrious, Robert or Rupert, who was a monk at the Benedictine abbey of Saint Laurent in Liège at the beginning of the 12th century, expounded a theory which was dear to him. The sea of brass symbolised the baptism, the twelve oxen represented the Apostles. Doubtless, this theory was behind the inspiration for the fonts of Saint Bartholomew's. It is obvious that the symbolism of Renier's work is virtually inexhaustible. S. Balau and L. Halkin clearly revealed a triple symbolism in the slightly enigmatic inscription on the lower rim of the bowl. The oxen of the sea of brass, thought to represent the Apostles, could also represent their successors, the Bishops of Liège. As for the « river », that could be both the Jordan and the waters of the fonts.

**The fonts
from the 12th
to the 20th century**

The fonts have been used for their designated purpose from
their creation until the present time, apart from an interval of
several years during the revolutionary period.

They remained at Notre-Dame-aux-Fonts, parish church of
the Cathedral of Saint Lambert, until 1796. In 1793 the Liège
revolutionaries had voted to destroy the cathedral. This
decision was put into effect the following year, but it took
long years to remove all traces of the enormous monument
and its various appendages, one of which was
Notre-Dame-aux-Fonts. Dismantled, the work of Renier of
Huy was removed on the orders of the Commissars of the
Republic.

Following the Concordat of 1801, the fonts were installed in
1804 in Saint Bartholomew's, now the parish church. The
works had thus survived the Revolutionary turmoil, but not
without damage. The original cover, on which were depicted
the figures of the Prophets and the Apostles, had been lost, as
had two of the oxen on which the font stood. The ten
remaining oxen were set down around the circumference of a
flat stone, without supervision and with no attention being
paid to the original theological significance of the way they
were grouped. Before the oxen could be repositioned in the
order described in the First Book of Kings it was necessary to
wait until the Rhine-Meuse Exhibition of 1972 and the
patient and competent labours of the restoration workshop of
the Schnütgen Museum in Cologne. During the exhibition a
new circular stone was laid in Saint Bartholomew's to
support the restored work.

**Renier, artist
and craftsman of genius**

The baptismal fonts currently housed in the Church of Saint
Bartholomew in Liège are dignified examples of the
liturgical magnificence of brass, its chromatic value, the light
and the gold in its colouring. The secrets of the foundryman,
the prowess of the craftsman, skills handed down from
generation to generation, all have been used by Renier to
achieve classic perfection. The figures have real depth. The
spaces have their own significance. Faces reveal feelings.
Serene and calm, man comes face to face with his fellow
man, to listen to him, understand him, make him believe. No
gnashing of teeth, no hideous figures. Just serene forms,
proud, muscular, nobly clothed.

Here, in this Roman sanctuary
whose twin towers
are a landmark of the Liège countryside,
the baptismal fonts of Renier of Huy
are proof of the skill
of a craftsman in metal,
of a perfected art,
of the gentleness of the Mosan.

The Shrine of Our Lady

or Classical Perfection

Nicholas of Verdun

Tournai

Cathedral

In the 12th and 13th centuries
Tournai was at the heart of the economy
of the Scheldt valley.
Like a great blue vein the Scheldt flowed
through the town and brought life to it.

It linked it with Valenciennes, Ghent
and the North Sea, and with the rich
pastures of England.
A network of roads
spread out from the river,
based on the old Roman routes
and serving the hinterland.

Tournai : a link in the international business chain of the 12th and 13th centuries

The subsoil provided the city with one essential raw material; limestone. There were the quarries of Barges and Roquelette Saint Nicaise, the lime-kilns and furnaces of Saint Piat and sclptors' workshops near the cathedral hose creations found their way tothe four corners of Christendom.

Wool was another important commdity. The great merchants, members of the Charity of Saint Christopher, ordered it from England and had it woven into cloth which was sold in Ghent, Genoa, Vienna, Venice and Milan.

An area of forty hectares (about a hundred acres) was surrounded by ramparts, and, within it, three concentric successively developed. At the centre was the most important, the episcopal zone, the focal point of the town and flanked by the port. Then came two municipal zones, bustling with industry and commerce and divided into numerous parishes.

A link in the great chain of international commerce, Tournai was affiliated to the Hanse of London and seventeen other towns. It took an active part in the fairs of Champagne and held its own fairs in May and September.
Between 1180 and 1280 the town was at the height of its prosperity, and an impressive amount of building took place. A belfry came first, a solid stone symbol of the freedom won from King Philip Augustus. The defensive walls were rebuilt and extended, and the citizens built for themselves and their descendants strong and sombre houses with firm and austere lines.
The clergy had the religious monuments magnificently rebuilt, and they also constructed a new cathedral. Its bishops designed it on the lines of the great royal cathedrals.

Stephen built a private chapel, a veritable casket of episcopal
power, and the Romanesque sanctuary. Obsessed by Gothic
styles, Gauthier, also known as Marvis, had the chancel
built.

**The Virgin Mary,
patron saint of Tournai**

The Tournai cathedral became the Cathedral of Notre Dame,
proof that the Virgin Mary was more important to the citizens
than God. She had been patron saint of the city since the
earliest Christian times, since the days of saint Piat.
Worship to her probably increased in intensity from 1090
when Bishop Radbo instituted a famous procession. In order
to free Tournai of a devastating plague, the bishop ordered
the relics of the Virgin Mary to be carried around the city. A
great crowd walked with the relics, imploring them, and the
plague was cast out and the city saved. Every year since then
the memory has been perpetuated and the cathedral becomes
the assembly point for the largest pilgrimage in the Scheldt
valley.
As a result of the same incident the cathedral has
accumulated a rare and precious collection.

**The cathedral treasury :
a fabulous collection**

The treasury of the cathedral of Tournai is one of the most
prestigious collections in Belgium. It includes works which
are important because of their great age, their beauty and
their quality, because of their place in the history of art in
Belgium and Europe, because of the part they have played in
the life of Tournai over the centuries, and because of the way
they have been venerated for over a thousand years.
The reliquary of Saint Eleutherius (1247) is almost as famous
as the Notre Dame reliquary. It is remarkable for its fine
craftsmanship, its wealth of filigrees and its Gothic design.
The Damoiseaux reliquary, made by a Bruges metalsmith
and dated 1571, typifies the elegance of the Renaissance
period.
The reliquary cross of the Holy Cross, said to be Byzantine
(6th-9th centuries), is remarkable for its great age and its
lavish decoration of precious stones.

There are also *works in ivory*, the oldest being a small
seventh century reliquary. The important diptych said to have
been the work of Saint Nicaise (c. 800) is probably typical of
the work of the Tournai sculptors who were influenced by
both ancient and Byzantine art and by the court of Charles the
Bald. The late 13th century *Virgin and Child* shows all the
gentle charm of an artistic trend which emanated in Paris and
swept through Europe.

Among the *liturgical ornaments* is a silk chasuble which
belonged to Saint Thomas à Becket (12th century), and copes
and chasubles which well illustrate the perfection achieved
by the embroiderers of the 15th and 16th centuries. Other
items bear witness to the lavish refinements of 18th century
art.

But of all the items in this fabulous collection the *Notre Dame reliquary* is the most venerated. It is also the most famous because of its quality, its place in the evolution of the metalsmith's art in the Middle Ages, and because of the craftsman who made it — a metalsmith of genius whose work is an almost ideal example of the wave of Gothic renaissance which was sweeping over the art world in the early 13th century.

Bishop Stephen commissions a new reliquary for Notre Dame

There is every reason to believe that the Notre Dame reliquary was commissioned between 1192 and 1203, when Stephen was Bishop of Tournai.

Stephen was born in Orleans. It was there that he first showed his talents as a builder, reconstructing the abbot's house at Saint Euverte, where he was abbot from 1168 to 1176.

He was abbot of Sainte Genevieve in Paris from 1188 to 1192 and again undertook many important works. He did the same thing in Tournai, and he was responsible for the elegant episcopal chapel of Saint Vincent, consecrated in 1198. It was the first Gothic building in what is now Belgium.

He carefully supervised the ornamentation of the cathedral. For the master-altar he had an *antependium*, or pre-altar, built, and he adorned it with thirteen silver statuettes of Christ and the Apostles. He also installed a vermillion reredos studded with precious stones. Unfortunately all this has disappeared. It may have been the work of Nicholas of Verdun.

The Saint Vincent chapel which Stephen had built shows that he was well aware of the « modernist » trend. It was no surprise then that he should approach a metalsmith as progressive as Nicholas of Verdun, who had already built up a solid reputation with his works.

From the date on one of these, the reliquary of Cologne, it is possible to date the work on the Notre Dame reliquary at between 1200 and 1205. Bishop Stephen did not, therefore, see his commission completed.

The Notre Dame reliquary is comparable in size to the great Rhine-Meuse reliquaries of the 12th and 13th centuries. It nevertheless differs from them in that its shape highlights its height rather than its length, like the reliquaries of Huy, Stavelot and Visé. This difference marked a change in the design of the reliquary which was no longer thought of as a coffin-like sarcophagus but as a chest which impressed by its size and its sumptuous decoration.

Length : 126 cm.
Width : 70 cm.
Height : 90 cm.

Who was Nicholas of Verdun ?

Though he is generally regarded as one of the greatest artists of the Middle Ages and the leader of the renaissance of the 13th century, we know little about Nicholas of Verdun. We do not know what were his links with Verdun, which was by no means an important artistic centre in the second half of the 12th century, nor do we know where he was born or where he died.

Two things, however, are certain : the date of completion of the pulpit in the abbey of Klosterneubourg, near Vienna, in 1181, and that of the reliquary of Notre Dame in Tournai in 1205. Judging by the similarities in style between the two works there can be no doubt that the Nicholas of Verdun at Klosterneubourg and the one at Tournai are the same person. On the basis of evidence in archives in Tournai it was assumed that the metalsmith settled in the city with his family and that one of his sons, also called Nicholas of Verdun, worked as a *verrier*, a glassmaker.

But it has been clearly proved since that the documents were misunderstood ant that the Nicholas mentioned in 1317 (not 1217) was not in fact a *verrier* but a dealer in furs (*vair*).

« Hoc opus fecit Magister Nicolaus de Verdun, contiens argenti marcas CIX, auri VI marcas. Anno ab incarn. Domini MCCV consummatum est opus aurifabrum. »

This inscription notes the name of the metalsmith (Nicholas of Verdun) and the date of completion of the work (1205). In addition, it points out that in making the reliquary the metalsmith used 109 marks of silver and six marks of gold — approximately 26.677 kilograms of silver and 1.468 kilograms of gold.

What is certain is that between 1181 and 1205, and more specifically between 1181 and 1190, Nicholas of Verdun worked in Cologne. The magnificent reliquary of the *Three Wise Men* in the city's cathedral bears the genius's stylistic stamp. It was started around 1181 and not finished until 1230, and not all of it can be attributed to Nicholas. But by its very design it is one of his works and he was personally responsible for the series of prophets which adorns one of the long sides.

**The reliquary
of Notre Dame
or
the Shrine
of Our Lady**

The reliquary is basically a chamber or chest made of oak, completely covered with metal highlighted with enamels, brown varnish, precious stones and rock crystal.

It constitutes an almost complete anthology of all the techniques the metalsmiths of the Middle Ages used and to which modern metalsmiths still resort-indenting, casting, stamping, engraving, sculpting, filigree, varnishing, enamelling (raised enamels, chambered enamels, etc...).

The original contents of the reliquary have not been preserved and we can only guess what was placed there in 1205. There is every reason to believe that it was something which belonged to the Virgin Mary, but, whatever the case, when the reliquary was opened in the 17th century, it was empty. As a result doubts were raised about the authenticity of other relics still in existence, such as those of Saint Ursula and the Eleven Thousand Virgins. An examination of the contents in 1856 confirmed the absence of relics of the Virgin Mary, but it is nevertheless certain that the cathedral had once owned them. It is possible that they were removed in 1566-67 when, during the Beggars' Revolt, the reliquaries were dismantled in a barn and sent to Douai. After restoration work in 1889-90, new relics, including those from both Christ and the Virgin Mary, were placed in the reliquary.

**The life of Christ
and the Virgin Mary
in fourteen chapters**

The iconography of the Notre Dame reliquary is not presented in a continuous fashion like a cartoon strip. Each scene is set in its own particular frame, but it is still possible to deal with them in « chronological » order.

We begin with the long side to the right of the end showing the Adoration of the Magi. The first scene depicts the Annunciation. The Archangel Gabriel, holding a phylactery on which is engraved the text of the *Ave Maria*, stands before Mary, whose form symbolises prayer and acceptance. Over the scene is the bust of an angel, 13th or early 14th century.

The second scene, in the middle of this long side, shows two
female figures in conversation. This is the Visitation, the
meeting of Mary and Elizabeth when each discloses a
forthcoming birth, that of Christ for Mary and John the
Baptist for Elizabeth. The final scene shows the *Nativity*.
Lying on her bed, Mary is about to receive the baby Jesus
from Joseph. The crib is symbolically represented by the ox
and the ass standing over a trough, while God the Father,
accompanied by two winged angels, gives his blessing.

For the next scene, one has to make a step backward in time, to watch the Adoration of the Magi. The sitting Virgin is holding the child on her lap, on the right side. Next to her stand the three magi. Two of them are offering presents to Jesus, who is looking at them. The magus on the right is looking upward and points to the angel who is bearing the star. The crowned Virgin looks rather like a queen, and it is exceptional indeed to see a crowned Virgin in a scene representing the Adoration of the Magi.

To continue in chronological order it is necessary to turn to the long side to the right of the end showing Christ on the throne. The first scene shows the flight into Egypt, and again Mary occupies a central position.

In the second scene Mary presents the child to the High Priest
Simeon whose hands are veiled as a mark of respect. The
public life of Christ begins with the following scene, the
baptism in the waters of the Jordan by John the Baptist. The
Holy Spirit, in the form of a dove, dominates the scene.

The imagery of the public life of Christ continues in the six medallions set into the long slopes of the top. On one side we see the Whipping of Christ, who is tied to a pillar and flanked by two executioners, Christ on the cross between Mary and

Saint John, and the Holy Women finding the tomb empty and an angel telling them of the Resurrection.

On the left of the other side Christ, raised from the dead, appears before a kneeling Mary Magdalen. In the centre He descends into limbo, where He frees the souls of the righteous, while on the right He shows Thomas the wound made by the spear. Convinced, Thomas kneels before Him.

The chronological sequence closes with the appearance of Christ on the throne on the end opposite that which features the Adoration of the Magi. The theme is treated solemnly and its significance is much more complex than is normally the case in the reliquaries of the Rhine-Meuse region. Christ is in the company of the angels, the imperial retinue of a benevolent God, and he carries a globe, symbol of his sovereignty.

The imagery of the reliquary is completed by the bust of an angel at each corner, by the bust of a prophet between the trilobate arches on the long sides and by symbols of the four evangelists in the enamelled plaques on the slopes of the top.

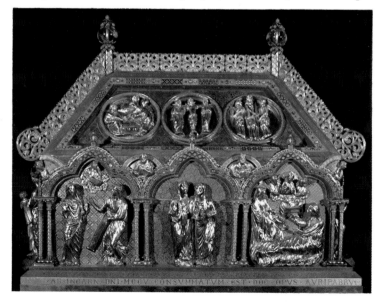

**The Notre Dame
reliquary
through the ages**

The reliquary of Notre Dame, which has always belonged to the Cathedral of Tournai, is currently housed in the cathedral treasury. In bygone days it was venerated behind the chancel, in the chapel dedicated to Our Lady of Flanders, a name which demonstrates the importance to the diocese and the province of the patron saint of the cathedral.

The cathedral chapter-house has always been responsible for the preservation and the safe-keeping of the treasure. One of the oldest of its institutions was in fact a group known as the Seven Sleepers, a term taken from the hagiographic legend of the seven sleeping saints. This team comprised two clerks who were responsible for the liturgical robes, two others who were responsible for the treasury and the relics, and three bellringers. All were sworn in by the chapter-house to guard and maintain order inside the cathedral. Each evening they locked themselves in the building where they had the use of two bedrooms and a rest-room or guard-house. It is known that during the 17th and 18th centuries the Seven Sleepers also had a « very vigilant dog which patrols the church by night » and was « tied up by day ».

1566 and 1567 were sombre years for the treasury. The chapter-house walled up in a hiding-place inside the building « ymages et aultres relicquaires d'or et d'argent » (statues and other reliquaries of gold and silver). But the Calvinists discovered the hiding-place and destroyed everything they found. On a happier note, the tapestries and liturgical ornaments were sent to Ghent, and part of the metalwork was put in safe keeping in Mons. The reliquaries of Notre-Dame and Saint Eleutherius posed problems because of their size. They were first dismantled in the straw of the capitulary barn; then, as the danger increased they were transferred to Douai in barrels which were supposed to be empty.

It was again threatened during the French Revolution. In May 1794 the chapter-house was forced to have a large part of the treasury's silver plate melted down, and in 1798 much of the cathedral's property was sold at auction. But the reliquaries escaped.
From 1796 they were hidden in various private houses and transferred from one hiding place to another to avoid discovery. Worship again took place in the cathedral after the Concordat of 1802, but it was not until October 15, 1804, that the to great reliquaries were returned to the cathedral.

Throughout the centuries the reliquary was subject to varying amounts of damage and certain parts were destroyed. In 1889-90 it was completely restored. Missing pieces were re-made, and the figurines, whose original order had been modified during 18th century restoration work, were returned to their rightful positions. Parts of the enamel work and the filigrees date from this particular restoration.

Certain statistics give us an idea of the importance of the cathedral treasury under the Old Regime. We know, for example, that in 1691 an order was made for 48.79 kilograms of silver for work on the font. In addition it is known that in 1794 the treasury was relieved of the equivalent of 124 kilograms of silver, 32.7 kilograms of gilt-bronze and 1.54 kilogram of gold.

Nicholas of Verdun, an innovator of genius

Nicholas of Verdun expressed himself calmly and discreetly, without pomp, but he fully displayed his innovative genius. His most important innovation, and one which clearly reveals the artistic changes of the early 13th century, is the way in which the scenes are constructed so that the characters seem joyfully alive and detached from the background.

Before then characters had been trapped like prisoners in their niches, modelled only in simple relief.

Nicholas of Verdun started a revolution. He grouped his characters together in tableaux which explained the psychological meaning of the scene, sometimes with great intensity. In the Visitation scene, for example, the implied dialogue between Mary and Elizabeth is rendered in the long figures, in their hands and their faces. His bas-relief characters demonstrate the independence of the statuary. It is possible that he used enamel at the base of the niches precisely to accentuate the contrast between the chest and the figures, since these two elements had previously tended to become confused.

His anxiety to create an independent statuary is very clearly demonstrated in the end on which Christ appears on the throne flanked by two angels. It can also be seen in the Visitation, one of the most impressive groupings on the reliquary and, in fact, in the whole of metalsmithing in the 13th century.

Nicholas of Verdun brings his characters to
life with the skill of a great classical artist.
These are noble, full-faced characters,
not actors looking for an audience,
but men and women living out
a profound drama
which was to affect all eternity.

The Goldsmith's Treasure

or the Gothic Prayer

Hugo of Oignies

Namur

Convent of the Sisters of Our Lady
(Exhibited at the Archeological Museum)

Solidly built at the junction of the rivers Sambre and Meuse is Namur, former county town, diocesan centre and cultural capital of Wallonia.

Like all towns guarding the strategic European crossroads, it has had a chequered history — sieges, destruction and military architecture have all contributed to its image as a citadel town. Nevertheless, its beautiful location has through the centuries helped it to preserve its charm and elegance.

Since the beginning of the last century the town has jealously guarded the most beautiful collection of consecrated metalwork in Wallonia, a collection of remarkable items gathered together during the Gothic era by the community of the priory of Oignies-sur-Sambre.

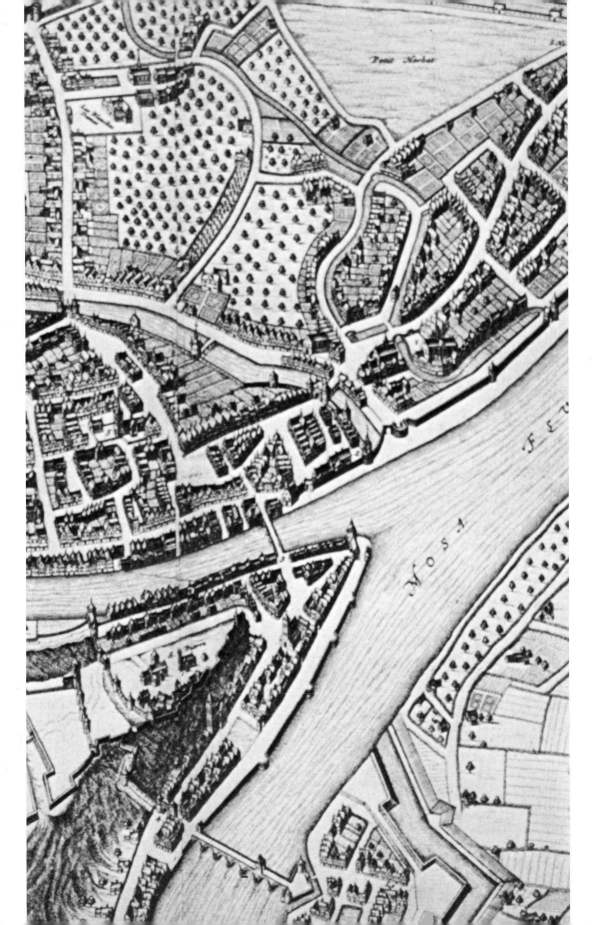

**The priory of Oignies
at the start
of the 13th century**

Currently housed in the Convent of the Sisters of Our Lady, the treasure comes originally from Oignies, a small Hainaut village on the banks of the Sambre, where a religious community was founded in the 13th century by four brothers. Gilles had been born in Walcourt, but he left his home town around 1187 following an unjust accusation.   He went with his brothers Robert, Jean and Hugo to Oignies where they settled on land belonging to Baudouin of Loupoigne, near a chapel dedicated to Saint Nicholas. Gilles, Robert and Jean were priests. Hugo offered himself to God in a manner which is described in the inscription in an evangeliary of 1228-30 : ''Hugo praises Christ in his work as a metalsmith. ''
He became one of the greatest Mosan metalsmiths and had a significant innovative influence on metalworking in the region in the Gothic period.

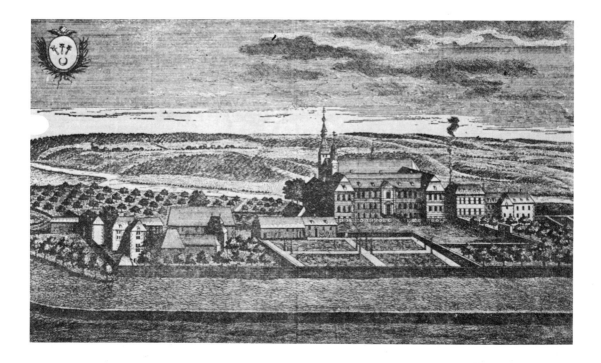

**Mary of Oignies :
inspiration and mystic**

The isolated location and the virtue of the founders attracted,
among others, Mary, the daughter of a wealthy Nivelles
family who settled nearby in 1207.
She was a mystic, a visionary who had access to supernatural
and celestial realities denied to ordinary people. Her qualities
and powers made her a much sought-after counsellor.
Her reputation brought many visitors to Oignies, including,
in 1208, Jacques de Vitry, a Parisian cleric, a learned poet
and a fiery preacher. At Mary's request he entered the priory
community and was to play an important part in the gathering
of the treasure.

**Jacques de Vitry
principal provider
of the treasure of Oignies**

Jacques' entry into the Oignies community was due to the influence of Mary. He also wrote her biography (*vita*) at the request of the Bishop of Toulouse, Folquet, who had similarly stayed at Oignies before the mystic's death. In 1213 Jacques preached in favour of the Crusade against the Albigenses, for whom Mary nursed a passionate aversion. From 1215 he took part in the Crusade against the Saracens. Appointed papal legate, he left for Syria and became Bishop of Saint John of Acre.

In 1226 he returned to Oignies and exhumed the remains of Mary, who had died seven years earlier. In 1228 he consecrated the church of the priory, and the following year, along with Jean d'Eppes, he was designated executor of the Prince-Bishop of Liège. Jacques de Vitry died a cardinal in Rome in 1240 and his body was returned to Oignies for burial.

From Saint-John of Acre, where he had been appointed bishop, Jacques de Vitry sent to Oignies several fragments of the True Cross, relics which were coveted by the princes and noblemen in the Crusades. The modest priory was soon as favoured as the abbeys at Brogne and Floreffe and the powerful collegiate churches of Namur and Walcourt. Jacques de Vitry's dying wish was that he be buried at Oignies and he bequeathed to the priory his cross, rings, mitres, a portable altar and a triptych. Through the attention of the Parisian priest certain items were added to the Oignies treasure which were perticularly significant to the political and cultural history of the West.

**Brother Hugo,
the metalsmith**

A manuscript text in a reliquary
shows that Hugo made the reliquary
and that the rib of Saint Peter was
placed there in the Year of Our
Lord 1238.

By his generous gifts he helped to nurture the talent of Hugo, one of the community's founding brothers.

Hugo was a particularly gifted metalsmith who worked for several communities, notably the abbeys of Fosses and Floreffe.

Hugo also made the evangeliary and the chalice of his brother Gilles, founder of the priory, and, most likely, the phylacteries and the double-barred cross. The Oignies metalsmith taught widely in the Entre-Sambre-et-Meuse region, which is why the collegiate church in his birthplace, Walcourt, possesses two marvellous examples of his work : a double-barred cross and a turret-reliquary.

**The treasure
of the priory of Oignies**

Most of the forty items in the Oignies collection were acquired at the time of Jacques de Vitry and Hugo. They are divided into three distinct groups — objects relating to the worship of relics, those relating to the liturgy of the mass, and objects pertaining to the pontifical celebration.

The worship of relics

Reliquaries represent about half of the treasure, since at that time relics were the object of particularly fervent worship. To make them accessible to the faithful they were placed in chests or reliquaries and Hugo the metalsmith made several of these.

Among the most notable possessions at Oignies, thanks to Jacques de Vitry, were several fragments of the True Cross, some milk of the Virgin Mary, a rib of Saint Peter, a foot of Saint James, a foot of Saint Blaise, a tooth of Saint Andrew, a phial containing oil from the tomb of Saint Nicholas at Bari and relics of Saint Margaret and Saint Hubert.

At the great religious festivals crowds came to gaze in
wonderment at these relics, to pray to them, to give them
offerings, to touch and kiss them. They believed that the
relics possessed supernatural powers and as a result the relics
represented a wealth of faith and generosity. Those which
came from the East, evoking thoughts of Christ and the
Apostles and the places where they lived, the relics of
Palestine, Jerusalem and Constantinople, were the most
venerated.

The phylacteries
(c. 1230)

Among the reliquaries are five remarkable phylacteries, small square boxes meant to hold religious objects. Four phylacteries are similar in size and shape, a square with four semi-circular lobes bordered with a string of pearls. Identical processes of engraving, filigree and repoussé have been used.

The reverse side features the outline of the saint whose relic is preserved, Saint Margaret, Saint Hubert and, on two of the pieces, Saint Andrew.

The fifth phylactery, that of Saint Martin, is larger. Circular in shape, it is surrounded by six lobes set off with precious stones. Its decoration is altogether more lavish, finer and more elegant. The reserve side features an excellent representation of the Virgin with Child, Mary in a coat whose tight sleeves are emphasised by the high wrists. The perfect harmony of this phylactery makes it Hugo's most accomplished work.

The reliquary
of Saint Nicholas
(c. 1230)

A crystal tube is mounted on the base of a chalice and topped by a bell-turret dominated by the cross. The crystal is circled with bands inlaid with niello and treated in Hugo's usual style. The base is decorated with four plaques, which have been made by using the same techniques. The work is admirable in its simplicity and sobriety. As a result of a substitution at an unknown date the reliquary now contains a relic of the Holy Blood.

The reliquary
of the rib of Saint Peter
(1238)

The crescent-shaped reliquary is set on a high column mounted on a circular base supported by three dragons. On the base are eight spearheads decorated with the figures of the Virgin Mary and four bishops, including Nicholas, patron saint of Oignies. Chased in the spaces between the spearheads are foliage, vine-clusters, hounds and hares. The crescent of the reliquary is supported by two spirals covered with leaves and vine-clusters. The main face of the crescent is set off by foliage, pearls, stones and cynegetic figurines similar to those on the cover of the evangeliary. On the reserve side the floral network is broken up by two niello plaques.

The central cylinder of the crystal tube contains a strip of parchment which notes that the relics contained therein were placed there in the Year of Our Lord 1238, and that Brother Hugo made the reliquary. This work epitomizes the art of Hugo of Oignies.

The phylactery of Saint Andrew
Diameter : 0,22 cm.
A wooden centre with gilded
copper on the faces and silver on
the edges.

The reliquary of Saint-Nicholas
Height : 29.3 cm;
diameter : 8.3 cm.
A crystal tube set in a base and
crowned with a silver cover.

Reliquaries of Saint Peter
and Saint Blasus

*Reliquary
of the milk
of the Virgin
(mid-13th century)*

A dove, symbol of purity and virginal maternity, perches on a small column mounted on a hemispherical calotte, itself supported by the paws of a carnivorous animal. The base of the reliquary is decorated by three quadrilobal niellos at the centre of the knots, and in them are the favourite themes of the day — Christ on the cross, the Virgin Mary and Saint John, all with affected expressions.

According to Barbier of Montault, this strange relic is galactite, a sort of white chalk from the Cave of Milk near Bethlehem where, tradition has it, the Holy Family took refuge. In the Middle Ages it was venerated in numerous Western churches.

Brother Hugo's influence can be seen in the detail of the work, in the use of the knot and in the general themes, but the technique has lost some of its elegance and lightness.

Reliquary of the milk of the Virgin
Height : 45 cm.
A dove in gilded silver perched on a column set on a hemisphere.

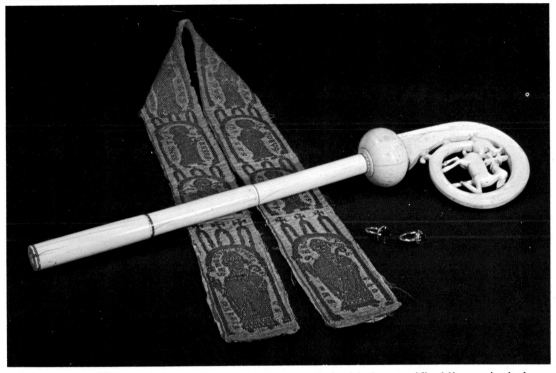

The pontifical celebration

Those pieces connected with the pontifical liturgy include a cross, rings and two mitres, one of which is unique, being made of parchment and decorated with miniatures.
These items were bequeathed by Jacques de Vitry and were probably used by him when, as bishop, he presided over the solemn celebrations.

The celebration of mass

A portable altar and a triptych, a Byzantine cross, another cross attributed to Hugo, and two items signed by him — a chalice and an evangeliary bound in a precious cover and containing the prayers said by the priest during mass.
The cross, the portable altar and the triptych all contained relics.   They were used during mass, especially when it was celebrated somewhere other than in the church.   The portable altar was also used outside the church when important occasions had to be solemnised by the presence of a sacred symbol.

The evangeliary
(1228-30)

First cover : Christ in majesty
The haloed Christ, seated, raises His right arm in a gesture of benediction and holds a globe in His left hand. His ample coat is made of overlaid metal pleats, and at the four angles of the central plate are symbols of the Evangelists. Four discs of chambered enamels highlight the base.
This central scene is separated from the silver foliage-decorated fluting by the inscription in Latin : "The book is written on the inside as on the outside. Hugo took great trouble with the writing. Pray for him. Other men praise Christ with their voices. Hugo praises Him in his work as a metalsmith, giving greater value to the writings by his labours."

Six niello plaques, set in the gold foliage decorated with clusters of leaves and cynegetic elements, form the outer frame of the piece. Within these designs can be found angels, dragons with human heads, Saint Nicholas and Brother Hugo, kneeling and offering his book. The border is highlighted by multi-coloured precious stones — garnet, agate, emeralds, amethysts and pearls.

Second cover : the Crucifixion
In the centre is Christ on the cross, slim, head bowed, flanked by the Virgin Mary and Saint John. Their clothing is identical to that of the first cover. Above the cross the sun and moon are represented by a ruby and a pearl.
The outer decoration has many things in common with the first cover, although there are no niello plaques in the network of vegetation.

The text
The 178 folios of manuscript are covered with Gothic writing (*textualis quadrata*). There is a single decorative element on folio 2 : in the margin at the start of the letter I. The foliage in this decoration is identical to that of the metalwork of the covers. This work is an example of the technical competence of Hugo and the maturity of the master in his harmonious use of vegetal, zoomorphic and anthropomorphic elements.

The evangeliary
Height : 32.5 cm; width : 23.2 cm; thickness of edge : 2 cm.
The binding consists of two thin strips of oak, painted red on the inside and covered on the outside by two partly gilded silver strips.

These niellos represent Christ on
the cross, the Virgin Mary, Saint
John and six Apostles, Saint Peter
with his keys and the cross, Saint
Paul with the book and the sword,
Saint Bartholomew with the knife,
Saint James with the sword, Saint
Andrew and his cross and Saint
Thomas and the rule. In their
clothing and their general form,
these characters are similar to the
figures on the evangeliary.

Height : 17.8 cm;
diameter : 15.4 cm

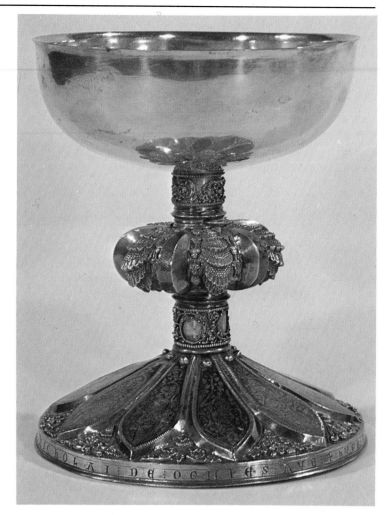

*The chalice
of Gilles of Walcourt
(1228-30)*

The smooth hemisperic cup is mounted on a round stem
broken by a ribbed knot between two filigree rings. Ten
niello plaques shaped like spearheads decorate the circular
base.

A Latin inscription runs around the edge of the base : "Hugo
made me. Pray for him. The chalice of the Church of Saint
Nicholas at Oignies. Greetings !"
The richness of the decorative vegetation and the discreet
sobriety of the niellos have been admirably combined in the
paten.

**Hugo of Oignies :
his inspiration
and creativity**

The evangeliary, the chalice and the reliquary of Saint Peter are three items which are unquestionably the work of Brother Hugo; all carry his signature. Beside them are other works, including certain phylacteries, which were made either by the monkmetalsmith or under his guidance, possibly even in his workshop. From all of them a clear picture of the originality of the Mosan artist emerges.

Hugo of Oignies was not a great innovator in the field of iconography. He merely followed the options and interpretations of his time and was content to borrow from contemporary imagery the themes of the Crucifixion, the Virgin Mary and Christ in majesty, and the representations of the saints and the Apostles.

The Crucifixion was a common theme. Its most popular presentation is in the cross flanked by Saint John and the Virgin Mary. On the evangeliary the figure of Christ meekly follows the new trends set by Nicholas of Verdun. Christ is dead, His head bowed, His body nailed to the cross by three nails. Mary and John are quite static and play only a small part in the drama. The presence above the cross of the sun and moon is common and is probably drawn from the Gospel which says that at the moment of Christ's death the sky will darken and the earth be shaken by quakes.

Christ in majesty is seated on a throne, holding a globe in one hand and raising the other in a gesture of benediction. He is surrounded by the symbols of the Evangelists. This theme has varied only slightly over the centuries, the seat has replaced the throne and the globe has occasionally been substituted by a book.

The Virgin in majesty is represented in a conventional way, but on the reverse of the phylactery of Saint Martin, Hugo has engraved an admirable figure of Mary holding Jesus in her arms. She has lost the rigidity of the Romanesque madonnas and acquired greater humanity. But the link between mother and child is still not particularly notable in a work in which the Remois spirit nevertheless already breathes.

The Apostles are represented by their symbols : the angel of
Saint Matthew, the lion of Saint Mark, the ox of Saint Luke
and the eagle of Saint John.
Saints in conventional poses are recognisable by their
attributes : Saint Margaret by the palm of the martyr, Saint
Hubert by the hunting staff and the keys he received from
Saint Peter, Saint Andrew by the cross, the symbol of his
martyrdom.

Brother Hugo's originality and creativity are most evident in
his marvellous marginal decoration. He introduced a
spontaneity and a freshness which were to be widely copied.
After him floral and cynegetic elements proliferated in a
variety of forms and with a preoccupation with the naturalism
which Hugo helped to introduce to metalworking.
One example of his originality is in the frieze of his
evangeliary. Flowers and vine-clusters are joined by slender
stems and arranged like an embroidery of plants or an
illustrated manuscript and animated by huntsmen and
hounds. It is a rare and elegant art created by an outstanding
decorator who had no difficulty in rivalling in metal the most
skilled of miniaturists.

repoussage
detail from the
phylactery of Saint Andrew

Hugo of Oignies, the craftsman

Hugo used numerous techniques popular among the metalsmiths of the Middle Ages — filigree, granulating, chasing, repoussé, stamping, niellure.

The filigrees were principally decorative, strips of gold and silver cut thinly and worked with small pincers into curbs, counter-curbs and spirals soldered at the base. Raised perforated filigrees were also used. The repoussé technique consists of hollowing out a deep ridge in the beaten metal, thus marking the limits of the area to be reproduced, then using special tools to work on the reverse side of the metal and give it the desired form.

chasing
detail from the tryptich

setting precious stones
evangeliary

Stamping allows the same notif to be reproduced *ad infinitum*. A steel mould is imprinted with the required shape in relief. This technique, used in large-scale works, has been adapted by Brother Hugo for his floral decorations. In this particular area the Oignies craftsman was an innovator. He deals with leaves, vine-clusters, stems, animals and people individually, skilfully retouching them and fixing them to the base of the plaque.

The enamelled decoration which was dear to the artists of the previous century had no place in Hugo's work. The glass paste with its iridescent tones has made way for the monochrome alloy niello. The metal is inlaid after heating and each trace is filled with a mixture of copper, lead and sulphur. After burning and polishing the metal takes on a primitive splendour, most noticeable in the reliquary of Saint Barnabas.

Niello is an encrusted mixture of lead, sulphur and black enamel used to inlay decorative patterns on metal.

niello-work
detail from the chalice

The treasure :
its changing fortunes

Mostly gathered together in the first half of the 13th century, there were no further major changes to the treasure of Oignies. Several works, including the reliquary of Saint Barnabas, were added in the 14th century.

There followed a period of wars and devastation for the monastery. In 1554 the French troops of Henri II descended on the Entre-Sambre-et-Meuse. The treasure of Oignies suffered, though the works of Hugo seem to have remained int act.

The first half of the 17th century was a traumatic period. In 1628 Rayssius compiled a catalogue of the relics. Oignies was once more attached to the new diocese of Namur which had been created in 1559. In 1648 the treasure was moved to Namur to escape the ravages of the foreign troops, mostly French, and a complete inventory was made.

During the French invasion in 1794 the treasure was hidden in a house in Falisolle. It stayed there until 1817, although several items were taken for churches in Oignies, Aiseau, Falisolle and Auvelais.

In February and May 1818 what remained of the treasure was placed in the Convent of Our Lady at Namur at the request of the prior, Gregory Pierlot, and with Joseph Lambotte acting as intermediary. It was he who, according to two letters written at the time, compiled the inventory. The treasure was accessible only to rare privileged people like the Parisian metalsmith Leon Cahier.

It was shown at exhibitions in Malines in 1864 and in Brussels in 1880 and 1888, and in this way its wealth and splendour were gradually revealed.

It was buried in 1939, a fortunate circumstance since at Whitsun 1940 the convent where it had been kept was completely destroyed by fire.

Unearthed in 1947, it has since been kept in a strong-box. The Sisters of Our Lady, who have conscientiously guarded it for more than 150 years, have placed it in the Namur Archaeological Museum for the year 1978.

A touch of freshness, refinement and elegance

The treasure of Oignies is rare in that it groups together so much of the metalwork of the same period, the end of the 12th to the middle of the 13th century, an era when the art of these regions was slowly evolving from the Romanesque to the Gothic.

It is also the only collection in Belgium to include so many of the works of a single metalsmith. And what a metalsmith! Hugo certainly used the conventional methods of the Mosan craftsmen of the 12th and 13th centuries, but he added a touch of personal freshness, refinement and elegance.

He was also an excellent draughtsman, as shown by the elegant figures in his phylacteries. The supple drapery and harmonious folds evoke certain drawings by Villard of Honnecourt, an architect of the Gothic era. From that time on the new spirit was to blow from France.

Hugo of Oignies is an ideal example
of the religious craftsmen
of the Middle Ages.
A member of a community
whose object was daily devotion
to the Lord,
his work was a permanent prayer,
a refined hymn to the glory of God.

The Mystic Lamb

or Flemish Realism

Hubert and Jan Van Eyck

Ghent

Saint Bavo's Cathedral

Ghent was situated at the junction
of the rivers Scheldt and Lys,
and in the 15th century was
one of the Western metropolises,
the largest town north
of the Alps after Paris.

Life revolved around the large-scale production of cloth and the intensive activities of the bankers. Industry and commerce were concentrated along the banks of the Lys. It was a remarkable area devoted to the urban way of life and sprinkled with prestigious buildings housing the ecclesiastical and civic authorities.

The power and civic offices were shared between three groups of citizens—the Patriciate, the great drapers, weavers and fullers, and the small trades, unalterably fixed at fifty-three and including everything from tanning to baking.

The parish of Saint John

The parish of Saint John partially overlapped the land on which the nobility had built their homes. In the early part of the 15th century there was intense activity in the parish church, which, from 1540, became Saint Bavo's Cathedral. On the initiative of Master Jan Van Impe, vicar of the parish from 1421 to 1440, funereal monuments were erected, the deambulatory of the chancel was completed and the side-chapels were built and furnished.

Joos Vijd and
Elisabeth Borluut

Joos Vijd, who was responsible for the direction of the
building of the parish church, and his wife Elisabeth Borluut
were members of the rich Ghent bourgeoisie.
Like his contemporaries he preferred to invest his capital in
land and works of art, rather than in the cloth industry which
was in a state of crisis and lacking in openings.
He acquired various properties in the Waasland, and, as a
lord of the Court of Walle at Beveren, built a hospital there
for the care of pilgrims.
A childless couple, Joos Vijd and Elisabeth Borluut gave part
of their fortune towards the building of the Parish Church of
Saint John. They provided the funds for the first chapel in the
south deambulatory, and their coat-of-arms was set in the
key-stone of the chapel and that of the adjoining gallery.
They financed not only the building of the oratory but its
furniture and liturgy. They inaugurated a daily mass and
provided the stained glass and, most notably, an outstanding
reredos.

**The creators
of the Mystic Lamb**

The altar-screen of the Mystic Lamb is signed on the lower edge of the four panels visible when closed by a dedicatory inscription in Latin :

*Pictor Hubertus e eyck maior quo nemo repertus Incepit.
pondus. que Johannes arte secundus (Frater) perfecit.
Judoci Vijd prece fretus VersU seXta MaI. Vos ColloCat
aCta tUerI.*

(The painter Hubert, who is reputed to have no superior, began this great work; Jan, second in the art, completed it at the expense of Joos Vijd. In these lines he invites you, this sixth day of May, to contemplate the work).

This verse has been the subject of many misunderstandings. The first word of the third line, *Frater*, is illegible as a result of 15th century translations and because of the unbroken tradition which says that the reredos was started by Hubert and completed by his brother Jan. In 1933 the collector Emile Renders tried to cast doubts about the authenticity of the dedication, but they were not taken seriously. It has also been wrongly assumed that it was written by Jan Van Eyck and that it was an invitation to people to come and contemplate the work. In fact it was a recommendation to the clergy of the parish to take good care of the reredos.

The inscription also names the two creators, Hubert Van Eyck, who began the work, and his brother Jan, who finished it. This double paternity has been continuously proved, both implicitly and explicitly, by the writings of foreign visitors such as the Dutch humanists.

De Beatis in his writings gives the reason why the second brother finished the work. Jan took over after Hubert's death, a fact which is not revealed in the inscription. Hubert was buried before the altar in the Vijd chapel and Jan in the Church of Saint Donat in Bruges, so there is no possibility of accidentally confusing the two.

Hubert and Jan Van Eyck

The Van Eyck brothers came from Maaseik, and it appears that Hubert was considerably older than Jan. We know nothing about his apprenticeship and little about his earlier works. When he settled in Ghent he received several commissions from the City Magistrates and such noblemen as Robrecht Poortier and Joos Vijd, but we know for certain only that he worked on the Mystic Lamb. He died on September 18, 1426.

Jan Van Eyck's biography is more complete. Though his brother was an independent artist, Jan first worked in The Hague from 1422-25 for John of Bavaria, Count of Holland and former Prince-Bishop of Liège. Then he went to work for Philip the Good, Duke of Burgundy. He settled in Bruges and bought a house there in 1434. None of his works for the two princes has been preserved but there remain several which he undertook for businessmen in Bruges, for the canons and the prince's staff. He also served the duke as a diplomat and was part of a delegation which Philip sent to Portugal to ask for the hand of Isabelle. Jan painted her portrait. He died in 1441, at the end of June.

The origins of the reredos

At an unknown date, but obviously before September 1426, Joos Vijd commissioned from Hubert Van Eyck an altar-screen which would sum up the bases of the Christian faith. A contract was probably drawn up detailing the two parties' reciprocal obligations, and in particular the time of delivery and the painter's fees.

Hubert used oak panels. First he covered them with a waterproof coating, a layer with a base of chalk and animal fat, or possibly parchment paste, which smoothed out the surface of the wood and allowed better application of the colours. Then he added the colours at varying thicknesses which allowed various degrees of penetration by the light. The colours were of mineral or organic origin and were mixed together with one or several measures of a drying oil base added to a material such as a natural resin.

The individual parts the two brothers played in the completion of the polyptich cannot be defined with certainty. The general conception is undoubtedly Hubert's, and he also painted the greater part of the reredos.

As for Jan, we can only guess at his role on the basis of specific traits in his other works, principally his innovative preoccupation with introducing three-dimensional areas by the use of perspective and tricks of light and shade. In this way he must be regarded as having been responsible for the scene of the Annunciation which has obviously been overpainted.

The original composition, conceived by Hubert and partly finished by him, foresaw arcatures similar to those of the lower panels and the shallow recesses where there were to have been stone statues of the Angel Gabriel and the Virgin Mary. Jan opened out the recesses and added a view of the town. He also tried to bring more life to the characters in the Annunciation whose poses clashed to a certain extent with their surroundings. The younger Van Eyck was also doubtless responsible for the panels featuring Adam and Eve and added to all of his brother's work modifications which were essential to the overall harmony.

A mason and stone-cutter were to position the altar and the sculpted stone canopy of which there were still traces in the 19th century.

The reredos was dedicated on May 6, 1432.

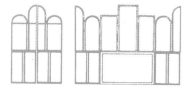

The iconography of the polyptich

The iconographic programme is without doubt the work of a number of erudite and influential churchmen. It illustrates one general theme, the Redemption of Mankind, the basis of the Christian faith.

It is impossible to say with certainty who were the men who inspired the programme, but informed guesses have been made at Arend Roebosch and Johannes van Impe, both Masters of Arts and at the time priests in the parish of Saint John. The latter was also the principal witness at the registering of the Vijd-Borluut foundation in 1435.

The iconographic detail is considerable and unique. In order to identify and interpret it, Latin inscriptions, often in decorative handwriting, were added to the panels and/or to their frames. They were addressed to the clergy who were almost the only people who could read and understand them. In addition, there have been several problems in summing up this abundance of images and symbols in a single concept. Originally the reredos was referred to as the Joos Vijd painting, then as the Adam and Eve painting, since the panels on which they were represented became particularly famous. Occasionally the « Eight Beatitudes » have been mentioned. In fact the work of the Van Eycks evokes two principal themes : the Redemption of Mankind and the Eternal Bliss.

ADAM NOS IMORTE PCIPUIT

EVA OCCIDENDO OBFVIT

The work comprises twenty symmetrically arranged panels. Its height, when open, is accentuated by the fountain, the altar, the dove and the full-faced Christ which form a central axis around which the other groups and figures are arranged.

Height : ± 3.75 m.
Width : 2.6 m. when closed,
5.2 m. when open.

The altar-screen closed

Towards the top the antiquity of the Old Testament is intermingled with the announcement of the Redemption. On the left and the right are the prophets Zachariah and Micah who, as described on the pennants surrounding the niches, predicted the coming of Christ the King. In the centre are the sybils of Eritrea and Cumae who, according to some medieval scholars, also forecast the coming of the Messiah.

Below this is the Annunciation, covering four panels. On the
left is the Angel Gabriel, kneeling and holding a lily branch.
His words, *Ave, gracia plena, Dominus tecum*, are painted in
gold, starting near his mouth and directed towards Mary.

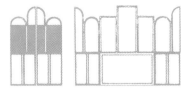

The three-paned window of the lavabo recess is also a reference to the Trinity. Several items in the scene are symbolic references to the Immaculate Conception of the Virgin Mary, such as the glass jug of water through which a ray of sunlight shines. A picturesque urban landscape, generally thought to be Ghent, can be seen through the window.

She is on the other side, kneeling before her prayer-stool. Her reply, *Ecce ancilla Domini*, is also in gold, but inverted so that it can be read by the Holy Spirit.

He hovers above the Virgin in the form of a dove. His triple halo symbolises the Holy Trinity, who determined the Redemption.

The four lower recesses are framed with small ornate columns and trilobate arcatures.

Stone statues of the two Saints John feature on the two central panels.

On the left is John the Baptist, patron saint of the town and the church, the forerunner of Christ. In his right hand he holds the lamb, wrapped in his robe and carried with deference.

On the right is Saint John the Evangelist, witness of God, who with a gesture of benediction exorcises his attribute, a chalice full of vipers. He is the patron saint of theologians and his Gospel and Revelations were to a great extent the inspiration for the reredos.

The two donors, praying, appear on the outer panels.

On the left is Joos Vijd, alderman of the town and warden of the Church of Saint John. He wears a suit of bright red wool, an example of the excellent products of Ghent.
On the right is his wife Elisabeth Borluut, member of a prominent Ghent family.

**The altar-screen
open**

Together, the five lower panels represent the Adoration of
the Lamb

The central panel, the Adoration, simultaneously depicts the
sacrifice of Christ on Calvary and the unbloodied repetition
of the same sacrifice at the altar. This is in direct relation
with the daily mass, the object of the Vijd-Borluut
foundation.

Towards the middle of the panel is the Lamb on a small altar,
the symbol of Christ who gave Himself in sacrifice for the
redemption of mankind. There are two inscriptions on the
front of the altar, *Ecces Agnus Dei qui tollit peccata mundi*
and *Ihesus via veritas vita*, and the altar itself is surrounded
by fourteen kneeling angels. The four in the background
carry the instruments of the Passion—the cross, the crown of
thorns, the nails, the spear, the rose branch with the sponge,
the birch and the pillar.   The two in the foreground carry a
censer.

Towards the top of the panel is a dove crowned with a
brilliant halo, symbol of the Holy Spirit.

In the foreground is the Fountain, an octagonal marble bowl
mounted on a bronze column and crowned with a statuette of
an angel holding two vases. This is the symbol of eternal life
and the grace acquired from the sacrement. The inscription
on the brim reds: *Hic est Fons aque vite procedens de sede
Dei + Agni*. The scene is completed by four groups of the
blessed on each side of the fountain.

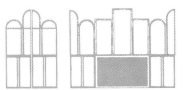

On the left are the patriarchs and the prophets of the Old
Testament. Among them is a figure in a laurel crown
generally identified as Virgil, and in this way the pagan past
is also represented.

To the right are the Apostles and the Church, the popes, bishops, deacons and laity. Here we can recognise Saint Stephen, patron saint of the church of the Augustine convent in Ghent which was founded by the Borluut family, and Saint Lieven, one of the patron saints of the town.

A little higher, among the flowering shrubs, are, on the left, the faithful and, on the right, the holy women. Among the latter group Agnes (the lamb), Barbara (the turret), Dorothy (the basket of flowers) and Ursula (the arrow) can be recognised by their attributes.

On the horizon is a series of buildings erected on tall hills and symbolising the holy city of Jerusalem, while further away is a tower which could be that of the Cathedral of Utrecht. To the left is a central building which is probably the Temple of Jerusalem, and there is a group of Gothic towers among which can be recognised the tower of Saint Nicholas in Ghent and, probably, that of the Gross-Saint-Martin in Cologne. Finally a group of Romanesque buildings whose architecture is similar to that of the Rhine-Meuse region.

The flora of this panel includes plants and flowers from various regions and different seasons.

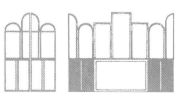

The groups on the lateral panels can be identified by the incriptions on the frames.

On the left are the Knights of Christ and the Righteous Judges (this is a copy), all on horseback and excellently representing temporal authority.

On the right are the ordinary people, hermits and pilgrims. Many attemps have been made to identify the characters, principally in the panels featuring the knights, but with little success.

Since the 16th century, however, Hubert Van Eyck has been identified as the first of the judges and Jan as the man with his head turned and a rosary around his neck.

The upper area comprises three panels which represent Christ, the Virgin Mary and John the Baptist. They have been called the Figures of the Deity, though in fact, this area represents an exaltation of eternity rather than the Last Judgement.

On several occasions the figure of God has been incorrectly interpreted as representing God the Father. The symbols are clearly Christological, the pelican giving life to its young with its own blood, the clusters of grapes, the pennant with the inscription *IHESUS XPS*. The inscriptions on the frames and on the stairs make references to the Holy Trinity.

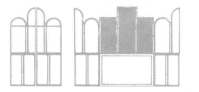

On the wide lateral panels are two groups of angel-musicians in choristers' robes.

On the left they sing near a lectern on which hymn books are placed. Saint Michael slaying the Dragon of the Apocalypse is represented in relief on the lateral face of the lectern.

The angels on the right carry instruments of the era, a small organ, a small harp and a lyre.

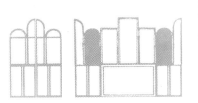

The small recesses in the narrow lateral panels feature Adam and Eve. The forbidden fruit Eve is holding is unrecognisable and whether it is a lemon, gourd, pomegranate or bitter apple has been debated since the 16th century. Carved in relief in the stone above them is the sacrifice and murder of Cain and Abel, the whole scene therefore representing both the causes and the necessity of sacrifice—the fall into sin, the crimes and misfortunes of mankind and the suggestion of the redemption.

**History
of the reredos**

The reredos was an integral part of the Vijd chapel where mass was celebrated every day for Joos Vijd, Elisabeth Borluut and their ancestors.

To ensure the permanence of this service the couple donated a large piece of land in the Waasland, and their foundation was registered on May 13, 1435, in the presence of the aldermen of the town.

It was envisaged that the Van Eycks' work should guarantee for posterity the religious service of the Vijd-Borluut foundation.

The shutters covered the interior surface and when closed the reredos was protected by a curtain.

Opening and closing was probably regulated according to the religious calendar. During periods of fasting it doubtless remaines closed. At other times it was opened only partially, the independent movement of the shutters making various permutations possible. During mass on Sundays and feast days the polyptich was revealed in all its glory.

The act of foundation of 1435 governed the management of the chapel and reredos until the end of the Old Regime. The parochial clergy, the Church of Saint John, the chapter-house after 1540, all were successively responsible. So, too, were the families of the donors. The descendants of Elisabeth, Joos Vijd's sister, who was married to Joos Triest, and the heirs of Elisabeth's brother Simon Borluut, took every care to ensure that the founders' wishes were carried out.

**The reredos:
one of the seven
wonders of Ghent**

The reredos of the Mystic Lamb found instant fame. It was
one of the curiosities of Ghent, known as the fifth of the
town's seven wonders *(seven antycke wonderen van
Ghendt)*. Every visitor with a feeling for art or culture had to
go and see it.

Everyone who saw the Van Eycks' polyptich expressed their
admiration for it.

Hieronymus Münzer, a Nuremburg humanist, saw it in 1495
and described it in the diary of his travels in a particularly
flattering way: *De nobilissima tabula picta as Ioannem cuius
simile vix credo esse in mundo* (the splendid picture
conserved at Saint John's which, it seems to me, is almost
unique).

The Neapolitan cardinal Louis d'Aragon visited it with his
entourage in 1517. His secretary, Antonio de Beatis, was
among a number of people who described the altar-screen as
"the most beautiful work in Christendom".

To Albert Dürer, in 1521, the altar-screen was a remarkable
work of incalculable value. But to view the reredos at any
time other than during a service, it was necessary to get
special permission, and it was for this reason that the curate
of the abbey of Saint-Pierre-au-Mont Blandin called on the
founders in 1433. A visit was arranged and it was the first
time that visitors paid an entry fee. These contributions were
collected in a chest, then deposited in a special account held
by the Receiver of the Fabric.

The changing fortunes of the reredos

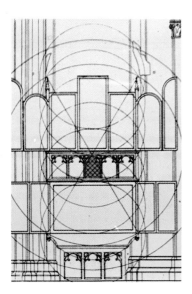

The Van Eycks' polyptich today occupies the same position as it did 500 years ago. It is one of the rare works of the Flemish Primitives which has been kept in its original situation. It has had its changes of fortune but it has always been returned to the Vijd chapel, a remarkable continuity which gives it an added dimension.

The Mystic Lamb has, however, been taken down, dismantled and removed on more than one occasion. Philip II wanted it for himself, but in the end had to be content with a copy made in 1557-1559 by Michael Goxcie. In 1556 it was locked in the cathedral tower to be saved from the Iconoclasts, and, in 1578, it was again hidden from the Calvinists. In 1794 the occupying French took the four central panels to Paris, and they stayed in the Napoleon Museum until 1815. The following year, six of the eight panels were sold by a French canon who acted outside the authority of his bishop. They found their way into the collection of the King of Prussia in 1821 and were eventually returned to Ghent in 1920 under the terms of the Treaty of Versailles. In 1934 the panels of the Righteous Judges and John the Baptist were stolen. The latter was found in a left-luggage locker at Brussels North Station, but the former is still missing. During World War II the altar-screen was moved to Pau. It was confiscated by the Germans and transported to Neuschwanstein and Alt-Aussee, to be repatriated by the American army in 1945. It was examined, cleaned and repaired by the Royal Institute for Artistic Heritage in Brussels, surrounded by a bronze frame and placed above a new marble altar in the Vijd chapel.

The Van Eycks: artists of genius

The appeal of the Mystic Lamb is in its humanistic conception of the universe. Man stands before his God with a new sense of his own value (M. Friedländer). The donors and the laity are as important as the Virgin Mary and the Saints, Adam and Eve appear together with Mary, John the Baptist, the Angels and eve God. '' We are far from the traditional representation of deliveration from the fires of Hell by the resurrected Christ, mankind at last redeemed. Adam and Eve have neither the attitude nor the appearance of penitent trespassers '' (Alexis Curvers).

The realist spirit of the reredos is also impressive. The Van
Eycks dared to paint everything in detail, landscapes as well
as faces (André Gide). Knowledge, experience and natural
science have been recreated by the human mind as if in a
miniature laboratory. Recreated too are the splendours of the
fabrics which were so dear to the Ghent drapers.
Numerous marvels of the elements of nature, and also the
most modest and the most discreet. Profound meditations
of artists of genius.   Homage to the art and the reality of the
senses (René Huyghe).
"The beginning and perfection in one" (Hegel).
But it is in the judicious and particularly skilful use of all the
ressources of the painter that the Van Eycks really excel.

In the polyptich of *The Mystic Lamb*
the Van Eycks recreated knowledge,
experience and nature as if in a laboratory.
Exceptional artists,
they opened people's eyes to a dazzling
new world.
With them the synthesis is close
to the point from which
the painting of North-West Europe
evolved.
(Elias Faure)

The Shrine of St. Ursula

or the Zenith of Urban Culture

Hans Memling

Bruges

St John's Hospital

Situated next to the Zwin estuary,
Bruges enjoyed astonishing prosperity
from the 13th century,
drawn from the sea and from
the water-borne traffic
which provided an
extension
to overland trade routes.

Bruges,
a Western Metropolis

In the 14th century merchants from all over Europe were to
be found in Bruges — Englishmen, Germans from the
Hansiatic towns, Scandinavians and Italians, Catalonians and
Russians — trading in English wool, Nordic wood, Baltic
furs, wines from Bordeaux and exotic Oriental spices. The
citizens held in their hands the gold and silver of the West
and a town grew up which reflected their riches.

Bruges was part of the vast state of Burgundy. The influential
Philip the Good built a beautiful house alongside the canal
and near the centre. He stayed there frequently, receiving
writers and artists, organising lavish banquets and rich
tournaments which involved the whole town.

Prompted by this display of ostentation the citizens
themselves enjoyed an opulent lifestyle. To invest their
wealth and demonstrate their power they rebuilt and extended
the public and religious buildings : the Church of Notre
Dame, the Beguinage, the belfry and the town hall.

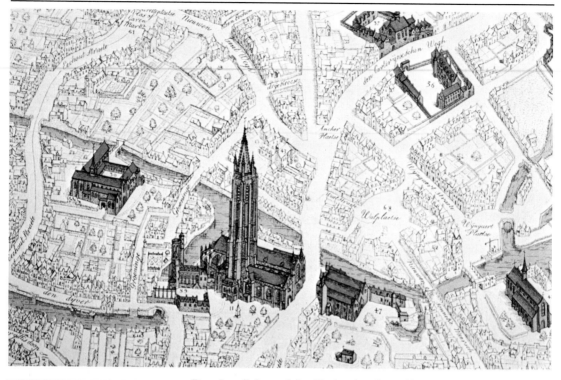

But the silting of the Zwin slowly suffocated Bruges. The English and German merchants moved to Antwerp, which offered them new techniques, and political activity began to be centred on Malines and Brussels.

Bruges gradually became landlocked, and by the 17th century all that remained of its glorious past were its magnificent architecture and its deserted quays.

The Hospital of Saint John :
an Asylum
and a Conservatory

As in other medieval towns, the citizens provided charitable institutions, and in particular one which is situated on the canal bank, near the ramparts and facing Notre Dame — a hospital dedicated to Saint John. Pilgrims, the elderly, the sick and the needy were all equally welcome there.

But the hospital also served as a conservatory, and in it were gathered together the various precious objects donated by Brugeois who were concerned with saving their souls. In this way they gradually furnished what is today one of the most prestigious museums in the town.

Some time before 1489 two nuns from the Saint John hospital, one of whom, Josine van Dudzele, came from a well-known and wealthy family, commissioned a new reliquary specifically to house the relics of Saint Ursula and her companions. They approached Hans Memling, a Bruges painter who was particularly popular at the time.

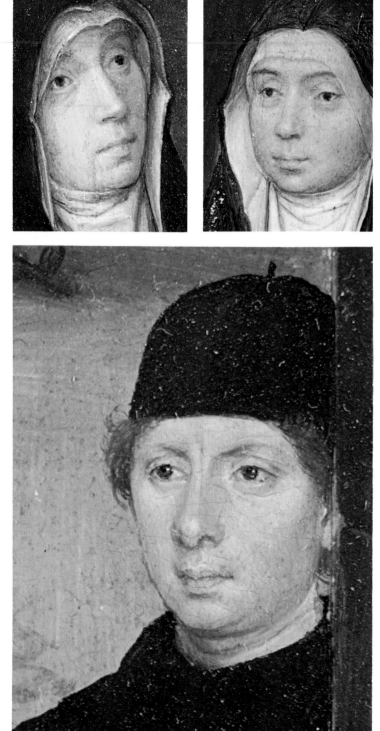

Born around 1433 in Seligenstadt, a little town on the Main, Memling left his home for the Low Countries at an unknown date. He apparently made his way to the studio of Roger van der Weyden, and, attracted by the wealth and the cultural and economic dynamism of Bruges, decided to settle in the Flemish metropolis.

He is mentioned in the citizens' register of 1465 : « Jan van Mimnelinghe, Harmans zuene ghebooren Zaleghenstat poorter XXX in laumaent ommexxiiij s(chellingen) groten ».
Before long he enjoyed an enviable notoriety, witnessed by his financial independence, his many pupils, his popularity among the wealthy townspeople and the comfortable estate he left to his three children when he died in 1494.

The work of Memling : a question of assignation

None of Memling's paintings is signed nor explicitly identified as his work by archives or contemporary literary sources. This anonymity was common in the Middle Ages where a souvenir of the subject of the work rather than of the artist was required. To establish a catalogue of his works it is necessary to resort to indirect references such as the style and the date. Certain works are dated, others feature personalities who can be identified from other sources.

**Dating
the reliquary**

As far as the reliquary of Saint Ursula is concerned there is no known documental evidence of the name of the craftsman who made the chest nor of the painter who decorated the panels.

The first mention of the work is made by Karel van Mander in his *Schilderboek* (1604). He relates that « the painter Pourbus could never grow tired of admiring it when it was exhibited on feast days ».

On the other hand, dating the reliquary presents no problem at all. In fact, a decree written in Latin by the lawyer Romboudt de Doppere recounts that on October 21, 1489, feast day of the Eleven Thousand Virgins, the relics were moved from the old reliquary to the new one in the presence of Gilles de Bardemaker, Bishop of Sarepta and Suffragan Bishop of Tournai. Also present at the ceremony were nuns and monks from the hospital, prominent religious and lay personalities and a large crowd of citizens. Forty days' indulgence was granted to all those who venerated the relics. Although he was an important citizen of Bruges, Memling is not mentioned as being among those present, nor are the craftsmen responsible for the reliquary named.

Since the publication of W. Weale's work on the painter in 1871 the illustrations on the reliquary have been attributed to Memling. There is no concrete proof to support this suggestion, but there is nothing to refute it.

Who was Ursula ?
History or legend

The daughter of the King of Brittany, Ursula's hand was asked for in marriage by a heathen, the only son of the King of England. As a condition of her acceptance, Ursula exacted a delay of three years, during which time her fiancé would be instructed in the Christian faith and baptised. In the meantime she would make a pilgrimage to Rome in the company of the eleven thousand virgins.

The pilgrims travelled via Cologne and Basle and in Rome they were received by Pope Cyriac. Full of admiration, he decided to accompany them on their return journey. The virgins were, however, unaware that Cologne was being besieged by the Huns, and, taken by surprise, they were massacred. The leader of the Huns was overwhelmed by Ursula's beauty and wanted to spare her, but she refused.

From this point the legend takes two different courses. The first ending is that the Huns, chastised by the hand of God, panicked and fled. Coming out of their besieged town the citizens found the bodies, recognised them as the virgins and organised a magnificent funeral. Then a citizen named Clematius built a basilica in their honour.

The second ending says that one virgin, Cordule, who had hidden in the hold of one of the ships, offered herself to be nartyred the following morning, but in vain. Some time later she appeared before a recluse named Helentrude and revealed the details of their fate. Since then she has been commemorated on October 22, the day after the feast of the Eleven Thousand Virgins.

The origin of the legend

The basis for the story is an inscription reputed to have been made by Clematius on a stone dating from the fourth or fifth century in a wall of the Church of Saint Ursula in Cologne. Edified by the martyrdom of the virgins, this Clematius had the basilica built in their honour. But the virgins were mentioned neither by name nor by number.

References of devotion to the eleven thousand virgins date back to the eighth century.

From the ninth century it is referred to in various religious documents, martyrologies, calendars, formularies, masses and litanies. The first of the virgins to be mentioned by name is Pinnosa, another daughter of the King of Brittany. Then Ursula appears at the head of a list of ten others. Her pre-eminence is confirmed in a Passion (*Fuit tempore pervetusto*) written around 975 at the abbey of Saint Bertin in Saint-Omer and dedicated to Saint Gereon, Bishop of Cologne.

During work on the ramparts of Cologne in 1106 a Roman cemetery was discovered near the Church of Saint Ursula. Word immediately went round that it contained the remains of the eleven thousand virgins, and the relics were exhumed to find their way to various parts of Europe.

That was when the legend was born, taking its shape and growing out of the names on the tombstones. Etherius (who was made the fiancé of Ursula), Pope Cyriac (who never existed), the bishops, archbishops and cardinals of Ravenna, Milan, Lucca and Basle (all unknown to historians) gradually appeared in the story. By the end of the 12th century the legend was complete, and in 1305 the Archbishop of Cologne designated October 11 as the feast of the Eleven Thousand Virgins.

As far as the Low Countries were concerned the relics went first to the Benedictine abbey at Sint-Truiden, from where they were sent throughout Belgium and northern France. Ursula, depicted clothed in ermine and with a halo, became the patron saint of orphans and, because of her protective cloak, drapers. She is called upon to ward off headaches and by people in danger of death.

Dimensions :
Length : 91 cm.
Width : 33 cm.
Height : 87 cm.

The old reliquary of Saint Ursula, which is still kept in the hospital, is small (19.5 by 28 by 14 cm). It dates from the end of the 14th century and takes the form of a painted wooden sarcophagus with a doubly sloping top. Ursula is represented haloed and sheltering her companions under her cloak, and she is flanked on one side by the Virgin Mary and John the Baptist and on the other by Saint Cecelia and Saint Barbara.

Memling's reliquary is shaped like a roofed stall with gable ends and a doubly sloping cover. Painted panels appear on the sides and on the top. The counterforts at the four corners are topped with small turrets and fixed to the central chest by pins. There are four statuettes, mounted on small columns and protected by a dais.

The long sides and the ridge of the top are trimmed with a pierced decoration of gilted wood. The sharp profile of the ends is softened by a wrought pointed arcature, surmounted by arches crowned with flowers.

Two series of three arcatures, semi-circular and set on small columns, frame the painted panels. These arcatures were in fact once a different shape and one can find traces of where they have been repainted.

The panel on which the Virgin Mary and the two donors are painted is movable and opens towards the interior. There is a certain harmony between the sculpted and the painted architectonic motifs. The motif on the arcatures on the end panels can also be seen in the windows of the chapel, while the motif of the pierced frieze at the cornice of the cover also appears in the painted decoration of the same cover.

On each side of the top are three medallions, the largest of them in the centre.

Each of the medallions has three different dimensions — the first that of a circle engraved into the decoration, the second the diameter of the medallion including the gilt edge, and the third the diameter of the painted area alone.

The imagery of the reliquary is divided into several distinct sections. On the long sides are six panels which recount the chapters in the legend of Saint Ursula. On one of the two ends the Virgin Mary and the two nuns from the hospital appear, on the other Saint Ursula shelters ten companions under her cloak. On the top are the six medallions.

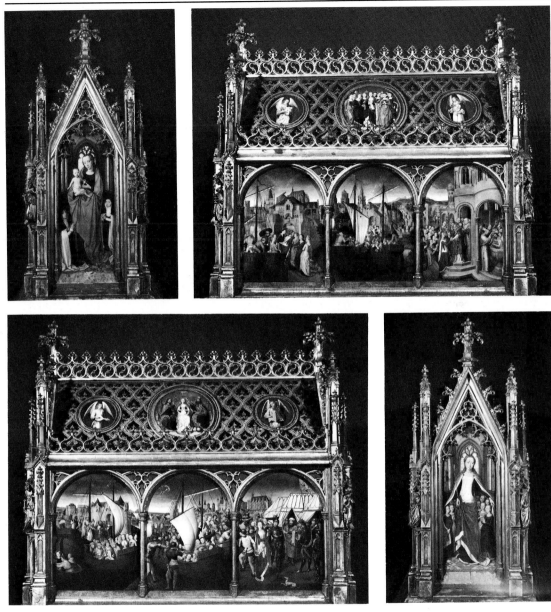

On the long sides of the reliquary
Memling tells the marvellous story
of Ursula, daughter of the King of
Brittany who, after a long and
arduous journey, was martyred near
Cologne with her companions, the
eleven thousand virgins. He deals
solely with the parts of the story
which describe the various stages of
Ursula's voyage, ending with the
martyrdom.

Part one : Ursula lands at Cologne. Leaving their ships and passing through a fortified gate, the procession enters the town. The hairstyles and clothing of the girls are carefully detailed. The monuments of the town have been painted with such precision that they can be identified. They are, from left to right, the Bayerturm, the Church of Saint Severin, the great Saint Martin and the completed chancel of the Cathedral of Cologne, still under construction. In one of the houses in the background, thanks to a carving technique reminiscent of medieval theatre, Ursula can be seen with an angel predicting her martyrdom.

Part two takes place in Basle. As
the sails are lowered the girls
disembark. Skirts gathered up,
scarves on their heads,
walking-sticks in hand, they are
setting off to cross the Alps, which
can be seen in the background.
Among the different monuments
depicted in an imaginary Basle is
one which appears to be the spire of
Brussels town hall, built in 1455.

Part three : the entry into Rome.
Ursula, her head covered by a veil,
and her companions — among
whom various male personalities
can be identified — are kneeling
before Pope Cyriac and other
leading churchmen. Inside the
basilica a number of pilgrims are
being baptised, while Ursula is
receiving communion and another
member of the party is at the
confessional.

Part four. After returning over the Alps the virgins, now accompanied by Pope Cyriac, a bishop, cardinals and other churchmen, rejoin their ships to *sail back to Cologne*.

Part five. Before they are even able to leave their ships in Cologne *the pilgrims are attacked by the Hun soldiers* armed with swords, spears and bows and arrows. Etherius, fiancé of Ursula, dies in her arms. The landmarks of Cologne can again be seen in the background: the Bayerturm, Saint Severin, the great Saint Martin, Saint Mary-au-Capitole.

Part six. Outside the tents of the Hun army *Ursula resists the advances of their leader.* Surrounded by armed and helmeted soldiers and facing an archer who is preparing his bow, she is about to die. The chancel of the cathedral makes up the background of this scene.

On one end of the reliquary appears the Virgin Mary. She is offering an apple to the baby Jesus, who is in her arms, and in the other hand she holds a flower. Her form dominates those of the two kneeling nuns, who are believed to be Josine van Dudzele and Ann van den Moortele. The former, having taken holy orders in 1478, was a prioress from 1489 until her death. The latter was admitted to the religious community in 1480 and died in 1496.

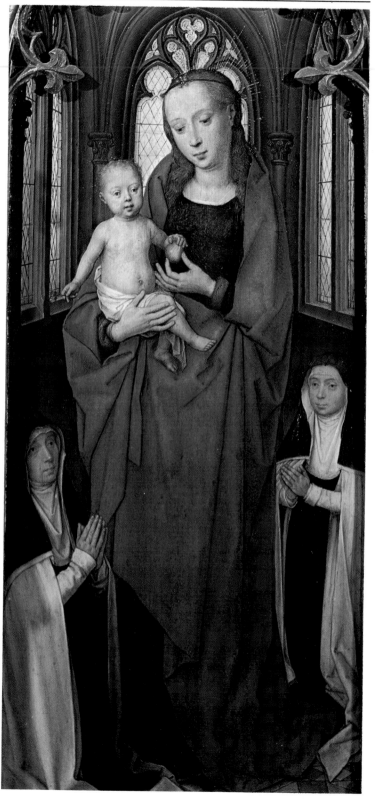

On the other end Ursula is featured. She is holding the arrow with which she was killed and sheltering ten of her companions beneath her cloak.

These two scenes are repeated in the same Gothic chapel, on the windows and the piers of the lateral windows. One comes right to the edge of the window, the other is set into it.

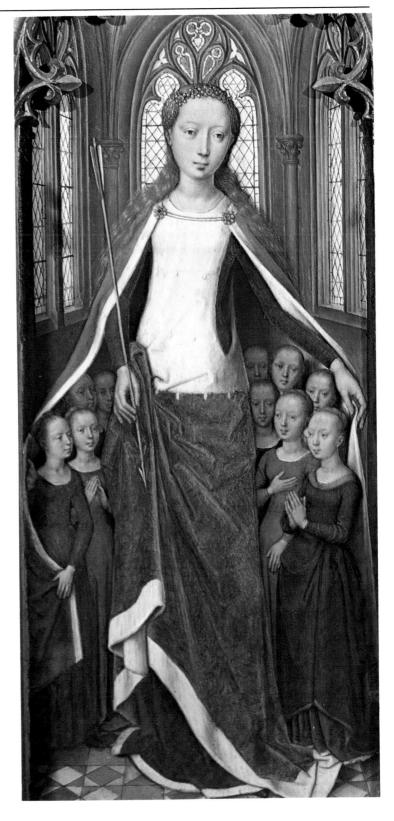

On one of the slopes of the top the large medallion features Saint Ursula surrounded by the virgins and other travelling companions — a pope's crown and a mitre can be identified. On the smaller medallion to the left an angel in an alb is playing a stringed instrument, while on the medallion to the right another angel, wearing a cope, is holding a viola.

The four statuettes at the corners of the reliquary represent four saints : Saint Josse (Judocus) with his belongings, a pilgrim's cap decorated with shells, a staff and a shepherd's bag ; Saint John the Evangelist, holding the chalice (along with John the Baptist he is patron saint of the hospital) ; Saint Agnes, accompanied by the lamb and holding the palm of the martyr ; and Saint Elizabeth of Hungary, carrying the crown and the sceptre (patron saint of hospital workers, an altar in the hospital chapel was dedicated to her).

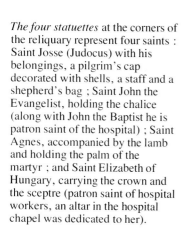

On the other side the central
medallion depicts the coronation of
the Virgin Mary, while the two
small medallions feature angels in
albs playing a lute and a small
organ.

**Conservation
techniques**

The painted panels were examined by Dominique Favart with
the scientific methods of Professor Roger Van Schoute's
laboratory for the Scientific Study of Works of Art at
Louvain University. The tests give some idea of the way in
which Hans Memling painted the reliquary.
Examination of the underlying drawings by infra-red camera
and reflectograph reveals a copious and detailed preparation
of the eventual illustration. Considerable research went into
the placing of the monuments, for example. Characters are
not side by side but grouped in arrangements which had been
reached after several attempts. By the time the figures were
painted they were in their final positions. The Wood Lamp
reveals a satisfactory state of conservation. Recent
overpainting seems to have been principally on the green
areas, the vegetation and clothing. The area which shows
most damage is the mobile panel on which are depicted the
Virgin Mary and the donors. On the slopes of the top an
underlying coat of gold over the whole surface has
maintained the distinct fluorescence of the black and red
bases of the medallions and the clothes of God the Father and
God the Son. Traces of renovation work are more numerous
on the top than on the other panels. The fluorescence
emphasises particularly well the difference between the old
golds and other golds, which have a distinctly mauve glow.

**The reliquary
through the ages**

Although it was meant to replace the original, the reliquary painted by Memling currently lies empty. But it originally contained a large number of relics, all mentioned in the removal decree of 1489 : fragments of some 15 saints, a relic from Mount Sinaï, another from the pillar where Christ was whipped, a thorn from His crown, part of one of the stones with which Saint Stephen was martyred.

Solemnly inaugurated on October 21, 1489, the feast of the Eleven Thousand Virgins, the reliquary then took its place in the hospital chapel.

It was transferred in 1839 to a room in the chapter-house which had been converted into a museum open to the public. In 1867 it was put under glass and mounted on a pivoting neo-Gothic stand made by the Bruges sculptor H. Pickery. In 1914-18 and 1940-45 it was taken to a safe place.

Along with the rest of the museum's collection it was transferred in 1958 to the southern section of the former sick room.

It went on display in Bruges in 1902, 1939, 1960 and 1976.

A prestigious work,
reflection
of an urban civilisation

In the painted panels of the reliquary of Saint Ursula Hans Memling reveals a remarkable narrative talent. His technique is full of subtlety, his details finely worked, his colours alive. The complete master of his art, he creates an aura of peace, meditation and composure for all those who view his work. Like a mirror, his scenes reflect urban life at the end of the 15th century as the citizens and merchants of Bruges would have known it. Reflecting his time, alert to the feelings of his contemporaries, Memling brings alive a legend which is already several centuries old by placing it in a contemporary setting : bustling ports, crowded squares full of activity, urban landscapes painted in detail.

With fervour and penetration he illustrated the imaginary citizen of the time. His towns typify all the prestige the residents and visitors knew, heavy decorative gates, solid towers and other works which are both reassuring to those they protect and imposing to those who look at them.

In Memling's creation is one last sign of the times and the society in which he lived. The reliquary is no longer made of metal, but painted. The citizens regretted the fact that non-productive objects were lavishly decorated with gold and silver. Precious metals were to be circulated and it was to painters that they turned for their symbols.

By his painting Memling the artist took the place of the foundrymen and metalsmiths of the Romanesque and Gothic eras, preserving the precise demands of those whose lives were already governed by an economy based on commerce.

Landscape with the fall of Icarus

or the Humanist Option

Pieter Brueghel

Brussels

Royal Museums of Fine Arts

Brussel's prosperity in the Middle Ages was due largely to its position on the Bruges-Cologne road, which linked the Rhineland with the North Sea.

Like all medieval towns Brussels was surrounded by ramparts, and within these great buildings were erected what demonstrated the power of the citizens - markets, town hall and belfry.

It first became a capital under the Burgundians, and, from that time on, the princes who ruled the Low Countries regularly established their seats of government in Brussels.   And so through the ages its appearance and its cultural heritage were to be dominated by its role and its administrative functions : its architecture, affluent suburbs, classical palaces, beautiful squares and museums were witness to the power of the citizens.

Of the museums those dedicated to the Fine Arts jealously guard a number of works of art of infinite value and intemporal beauty. Among these is the *Landscape with the Fall of Icarus* by Pieter Brueghel.

Professor Philippe Roberts-Jones dedicated a brilliant and exhaustive study to it in 1974, and it is from that work that much of the information in these pages has been taken.

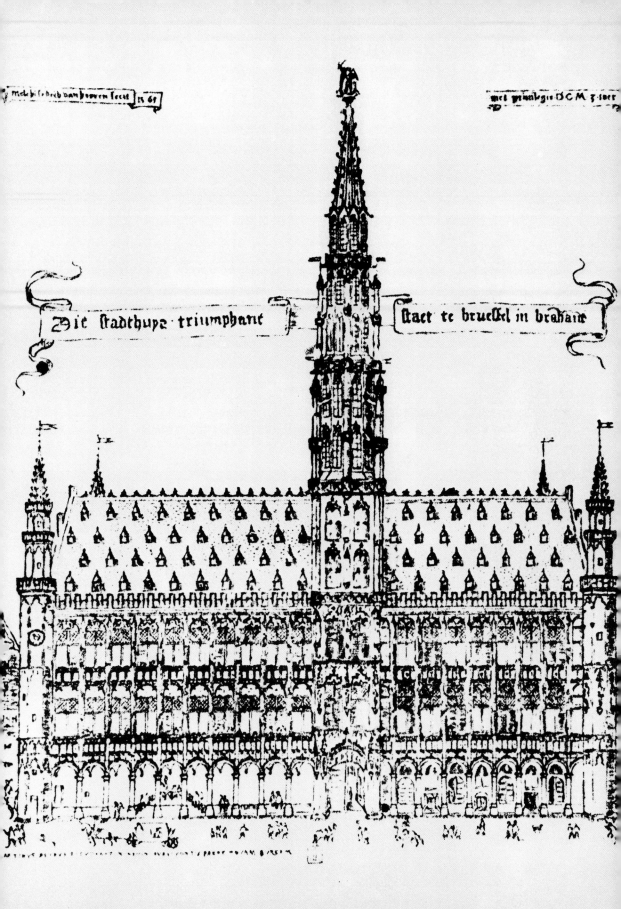

Melchifedt van Hoorrn fecit 1565

met gratie pgie DCM 3 Iaer

Die stadthupe triumphant

staet te bruessel in brabant

The story of Icarus

The Latin poet Ovid told the story in Chapter VIII of his *Metamorphoses*.

The architect Dedalus and his son Icarus were prisoners of Minos, the king of Crete. They wanted to escape, and since sea and land routes were forbidden to them, they planned to escape by air.

Dedalus built wings of feathers and wax and taught his son how to fly. "Take the middle route," he advised him. "If you fly too low the humidity will make your wings heavy. Too high and the heat will burn them." Icarus took flight and, intoxicated by the experience, defied gravity and approached the sun. The wax melted, the feathers fell apart, Icarus called out to his father, then sank into the waves.

An original interpretation of the myth of Icarus

The myth of Icarus is an old tale, often told and well-known by Brueghel's contemporaries. Brueghel did not simply illustrate the fable. He gave it new meaning, setting it in everyday life.

Dedalus is missing and Icarus is little more than a speck. The principal characters in the story make way for men absorbed in their day-to-day tasks to whom Brueghel has given pride of place.

Auden says that just as if they were at their leisure the characters turn their backs on the disaster.

We will never know if the farmworker heard Icarus's cry or the splash, which was perhaps as well since his end was banal.

"The sun was shining, as it must," the green branches casting their shadows.

Auden adds that the ship must have seen "this child falling from the sky," but it has somewhere to go so it continues calmly on its way.

W.H. Auden, *Museum of Fine Arts, in The Collected Poetry of W.H. Auden*, New York, 1945).

Who was Brueghel ?

The *Landscape with the Fall of Icarus* is as much the story of the man who painted it - Brueghel, the artist and visionary who still appeals to us today.

The early years
We know neither where nor when Brueghel was born, but it must have been sometime between 1525 and 1530. It may have been at Breda, in Northern Brabant, or Bruegel, north of Eindhoven and about 60 miles from Antwerp, or possibly at Kleine or Grote Brogel in the Belgian province of Limburg and near Bree, which in the 15th and 16th centuries was known as Breda.

According to Karel Van Mander, Brueghel served his apprenticeship as a painter with Pieter Coecke van Aalst around 1545, but there are serious doubts about this theory. What is certain, however, is that in 1550 he worked with Pieter Balten on a reredos commissioned by the Malines Glovemakers' Corporation. In 1551 he became a freemason in the Guild of Saint Luke in Antwerp.

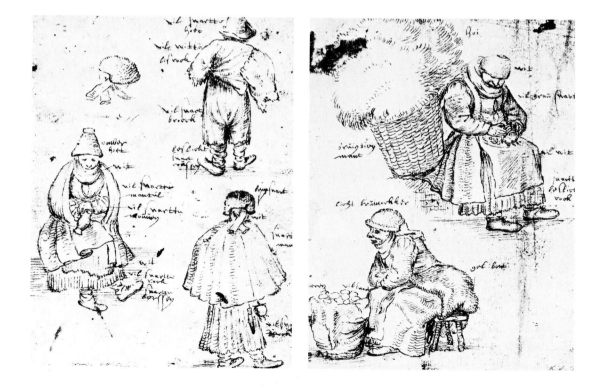

Of his social background, we know nothing either.
According to some theorists he was the son of peasants and
was born and brought up amongst them, which would
explain his sympathy for them. Other people, among them
Glück, believe his culture could only have been gained
through an urban upbringing. It is possible that he was born
into a peasant family and educated in a nearby town.

But he also travelled through the countryside, loving to meet his peasant brothers. From his encounters with the rural community he recorded some moving moments - the joys and festivities of the village, its labours and its sorrows. With Brueghel the countryside ceased merely to be decorative and, like the town, had its own nobility and values.

The journey to Italy

Like many painters and men of letters of his time, Brueghel travelled to Italy.

The numerous sketches and drawings he made on his journey make it possible to trace his approximate itinerary. He travelled via the Rhone Valley, journeyed down the peninsula as far as the Straits of Messina, visited Naples and stayed in Rome, where he met the Mecaenas, members of the high clergy, intellectuals and artists. Then he travelled back via the Alpine route.

While in Italy he paid no attention to the collections or the ancient ruins. What he loved most were the peace of the sun-drenched quays and the spectacle of the Alps. In careful detail he recorded their many different aspects and their exact nature. The Ripa Grande in Rome, the Straits of Messina, a view of Reggio and a panorama of Naples were all indelible, dazzling images. They were vibrant impressions eternally imprinted in his memory, and they constantly recurred in his subsequent work.

Brueghel in Antwerp

On his return in 1554 Brueghel settled in Antwerp, a cosmopolitan town rich in encounters and exchanges and one of the West's most important art markets.

He worked on the series of *Great Landscapes* which were engraved by Hieronymus Cock, a printseller whose laboratory was one of the most active in the Low Countries. Still working for Cock he designed the *Seven Deadly Sins* series, engraved by Pieter Van der Heyden in 1558, and the series of the *Seven Virtues* in 1559-60, engraved by Philippe Galle.

But Brueghel was not only a designer. He was a painter and his oldest signed painting is dated 1553. However, it was not until 1559 that his paintings began to appear regularly. In them he explained a vision of the universe, of man and of things which bears witness to his intelligence and his exceptional powers of observation and plastic expression.

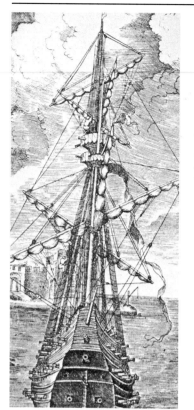

In the port he marvelled at the ocean-going ships and observed at length their refined lines and robust structure.

In his *Landscape with the Fall of Icarus* Brueghel painted a superb sailing ship with such precision that it can be recognised as a Portuguese four-master of about one thousand tons, the kind which sailed the seas between 1540 and 1600. Such is the detail that the crew can be seen preparing to drop anchor.

Brueghel in Brussels

Brueghel left Antwerp in 1563 and moved to Brussels, the political centre of the Low Countries. According to Van Mander, the painter's change of residence was due to his marriage to Mayken Coecke, the daughter of his former teacher, but more than one historian is of the opinion that there are more profound religious and philosophical reasons for the move.

In Antwerp he was part of a particularly progressive intellectual and cultural circle which was open to new and independent ideas on beliefs and the official Orthodoxy. Among his friends were the German Hans Franckert, who had been forced to flee from his home in Nuremburg because of his religious beliefs, Frans Hogenberg and Jan Rademacker, who had both been converted to Protestantism, Abraham Ortelius, D.V. Coornaert, Christopher Plantin and Robert Goltzius, all members of a group of humanists which had become almost a sect.

But around 1560 the group was disturbed by the Inquistion. In 1561 Plantin feigned bankruptcy and went into exile in Paris. Brueghel also left the Metropolis in 1563 and settled in Brussels, in the centre of a bourgeois quarter in a house which is now 131, Rue Haute. His first son, Pieter, was born there in 1564. Known as Brueghel the Younger, he specialised in imitations and copies of his father's work. A second son, Jan, known as Brueghel de Velours, was born in 1568. He became a friend and collaborator of Rubens and married the daughter of David Teniers the Younger.

Brueghel died in September 1569 when he was working on paintings commissioned by the town of Brussel. He was buried in Notre Dame de la Chapelle, where he had been married six years earlier. His wife, who died in 1578, was buried beside him and their son Jan had a monument built to them which is still in the church.

The Fall of Icarus :
a painting
with a cloudy history

The origins and the life story of the *Landscape with the Fall of Icarus* are unknown.
Several dates have been suggested — 1555, 1558 and 1562-63 — but as far as its conservation and changing fortunes are concerned there is no information.
it is possible that during the 17th century it was part of the Habsburgs' Collection in Vienna, but all that is known for certain is that it appeared on the art market in 1912.

Brueghel's Icarus
fell in the spring
when the whole pageant of the year
was bustling with life.

Near the sea
a farmer worked in his field,
bent over his plough,
sweating under the sun
which melted the wax of the wings.

Just offshore
there was a splash
which was of little importance,
and Icarus drowned.

According to W.C. Williams, in his *Landscape with the Fall of Icarus* (*Pictures from Brueghel and other poems*, Norfolk, 1962).

**The Landscape
with the Fall of Icarus**

In the foreground is a labourer, an impersonal, powerful figure painted on simple lines and in threequarter profile. He treads the earth with his weary feet and guides a wheeled plough pulled by an old horse calmly following furrows which are already traced. At the side is " a sword driven through a purse, a symbol of man's folly " (Ch. de Tolnay). At the far end of the field is the head of a man lying down, an allusion to the proverb " no plough stops for a dying man ".

Then come trees. Through their sunlit foliage are tall cliffs. At the foot of the cliffs is a port town built in the Mediterranean style, and ships sail towards it on a calm sea. Between the field and the port is a mysterious island, a sort of fortress which is probably a reference to the island of Crete where Dedalus and Icarus were prisoners.

Though smaller than the ploughman, the shepherd occupies the geometric centre of the picture. Surrounded by his flock and accompanied by his dog, he leans on his crook and looks up towards the sky.

**Composition
of the painting**

A mysterious and powerful microcosm, the *Landscape with the Fall of Icarus* reveals two distinct worlds where the reality and the dream confront each other and constantly intermingle. On the left is everyday labour, on the right a fantastic dream. There are no barriers between them.

Dimensions : Height : 73.5 cm
            Width : 1.12 m

On the right of the picture a patridge perches on a withered bush and there is the rear view of a fisherman. The drowning Icarus is represented by two legs, a hand and a few falling feathers, and nearby a superb sailing ship prepares to drop anchor. Top right are cliffs and buildings rising out of a mountainside.

On the horizon is the sun, the zenith for Icarus, but it is impossible to say whether it is rising or setting.

The eye takes it all in at will, captivated by the massive figure of the ploughman, drifting towards the shepherd and his sheep, sailing off towards the island, meeting several ships and finally reaching the port. It has seen nothing to surprise it on its journey apart from a dagger, a sword and a man's head. But it returns to the shepherd and discovers a fantastic scene. A man is drowning, feathers fly, water shines as if by magic, fairy castles rise from cliffs, a sun which lights up the horizon is reflected in the sea. Among these strange elements a fisherman and a ship bring us back to reality.

There is no juxtaposition. Everything is related in this universe in which one cannot be sure where dream ends and where reality begins.

In the foreground is the ploughman and behind him the sun.
Between the two, in the centre of the picture, the shepherd
around which everything revolves. Diagonals meet where the
shepherd, absorbed in his thoughts, fulfils his ordinary
duties. Oblique lines join man's activity to the dazzlin
heavenly body. Verticals such as the shepherd, pleats in
clothing, tree-trunks and masts break it all up. Colours,
design techniques, careful management and refined skills are
all used by this exceptional creator of genius. Synthesis of a
complex reality almost impossible to capture, the picture
amazes by its coherence and its legibility.

**What Brueghel
wanted to say**

In the 16th century Icarus was a symbol of excess and lack of
reason. Moralists accused him of arrogance, popular wisdom
stigmatised his ambition.
But Brueghel gave his failure a greater significance. He was
no doubt suggesting that gaining his freedom costs man
dearly, that in general the attempt to gain it not only ends in
tragedy but is swamped in the indifference of everyday life.
He said too that the working life has its own honour, that
nature is a generous mother provided it is greatly revered,
that the revelations of the world are inexhaustible and that
man will never cease learning about them.

Brueghel uses his brush like a philosopher uses his pen. He presents us with a total vision of beings and things, of life and of the universe.

The work of a thinker as much as of an artist, his *Landscape with the Fall of Icarus* offers a cosmic vision of reality which still speaks to us today.

The Descent from the Cross

or Mastery of the Baroque

Peter-Paul Rubens

Antwerp

Cathedral

It was from the 15th century onwards that Antwerp gradually became the metropolis of the Low Countries and a leading international port.

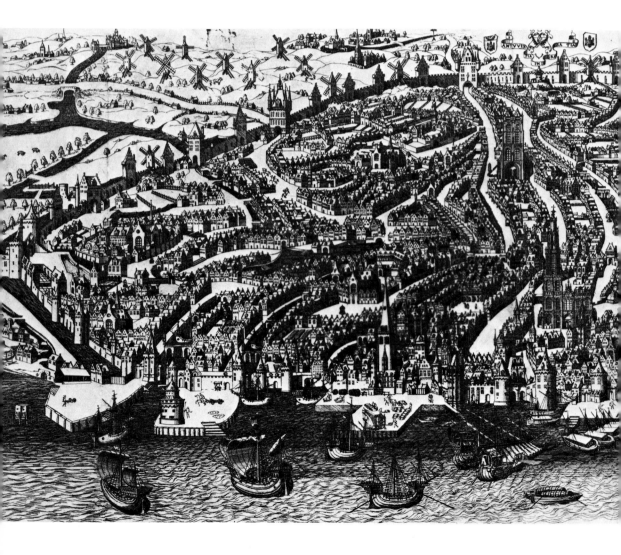

Its economic dynamism gave rise to intense intellectual and artistic activity.

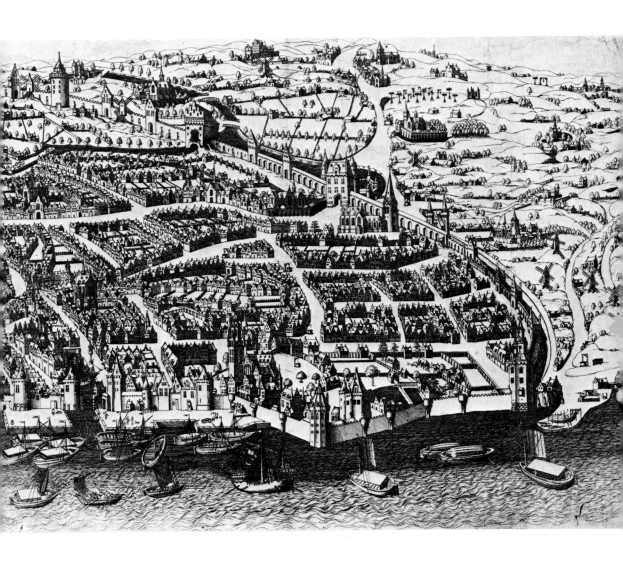

But the political and religious revolt against Philip II of Spain interrupted its progress in 1585. The Northern Low Countries declared their independence while the South remained under Spanish rule. Despite the closure of the Scheldt by the North, Antwerp continued to be an important commercial and artistic centre, directed mainly towards Spain, Italy and the domestic market.

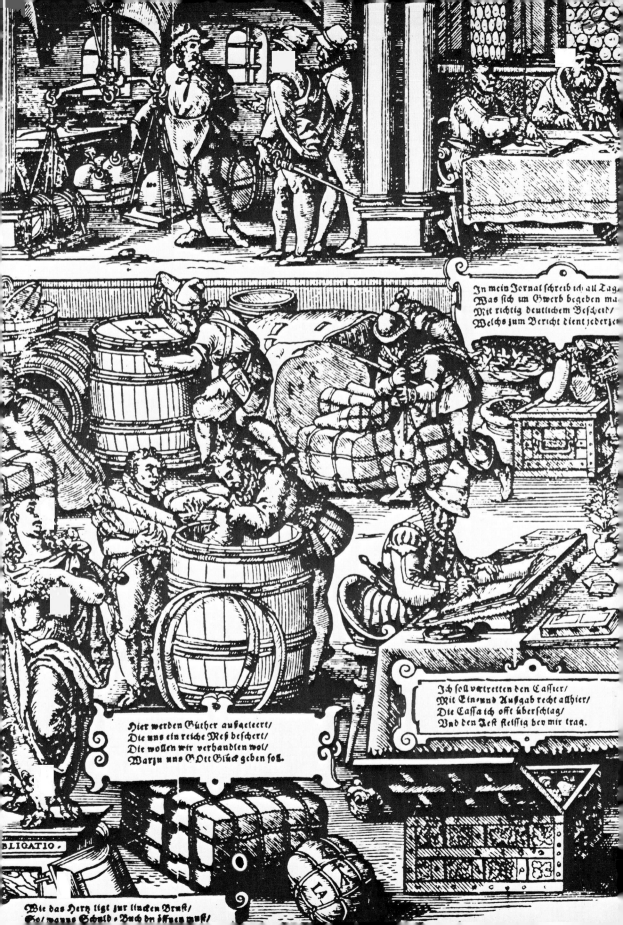

In mein Jornal schreib ich all Tag/
Was sich um Gwerb begeben mag/
Mit richtig deutlichem Bescheid/
Welchs zum Bericht dient jederzeit.

Ich soll vertretten den Cassier/
Mit Ein und Außgab recht allhier/
Die Cassa ich offt überschlag/
Vnd den Rest fleissig bey mir trag.

Hier werden Güther außgeleert/
Die uns ein reiche Meß beschert/
Die wollen wir verhandlen wol/
Warzu uns GOtt Glück geben soll.

OBLIGATIO.

Wie das Hertz ligt zur lincken Brust/
So wann Schuld-Buch du öffnen must/

Merchants, magistrates, guild and corporations publicised
their success by showing off their wealth. The great
altar-screens and paintings were realised for them and
became objects of investment and personal satisfaction. The
art cabinet became a sign of power and an object of prestige.
In Antwerp art was also a marketable commodity.
It was in this cosmopolitan atmosphere that Peter-Paul
Rubens was to grow up.

Who was Rubens ?

Peter-Paul Rubens was born in 1577 at Siegen in Germany where his father, a former Antwerp alderman, had been forced into exile because of his religious convictions. His father died when he was only ten and his mother returned to Antwerp.

At school Peter-Paul acquired a solid, all-round education which included Latin. He also learned to draw and copied illustrations from the Bible. Among his fellow scholars was Balthazar Moretus, the future inspiration of the Plantin printing shop. Rubens wanted to be a painter and as a result worked in the studios of the Antwerp masters. There he learned the rudiments of his craft, the intimacy with the materials, the demands of painting in oils.

BALTHASAR MORETVS ANTVERPIENSIS
TYPOGRAPHVS REGIVS CELEBERRIMVS,
CHRISTOPHORI PLANTINI EX FILIA NEPOS,
IOANNIS MORETI FILIVS.
Vixit annos LXVII. Deuixit VIII. Iulij. M. DC. XLI.

At the age of twenty-one, having been accepted to the Guild of Painters, he undertook the traditional educational voyage to Italy. For eight years he based himself at the court of Mantua and travelled throughout the peninsula. For the court he made copies of the famous works and this gave him the opportunity to practise and assimilate the themes then in fashion.

When he returned, official
recognition awaited him. Archduke
Albert and Isabella commissioned
their portrait and suggested that he
move to Brussels to become court
painter.

But Rubens preferred to settle in
Antwerp where he married Isabella
Brant, daughter of a rich lawyer,
and built up a network of social
contacts.

Commissions were soon pouring in and Rubens became wealthy. He bought a large house near the Meir and turned it into a patrician residence. He set up his studio there and it was visited by the greatest men of the time. There he carried out a series of large canvases commissioned by the rich citizens of the town, the powerful princes and the new religious orders which sprang from the Counter-Reformation.

In 1615 the Jesuits entrusted him with part of the decoration of the Church of Saint Charles Borromeus, which they had recently undertaken to build.
To Protestant suspicions of religious imagery, the Counter-Reformers preached representation and decoration, a marble temple symbolising Paradise, appealing to all the senses and transforming the liturgy into a vast spectacle capable of touching the emotions.

Maison Hibverue a Anuers dit l Gostel Rubens 1684.

During this decoration Rubens completed his first great
work, forty scenes which decorated the ceilings and which
disappeared during a fire in 1718, the first model for the altar
and the designs for a number of coats-of-arms.

The work of Rubens

After decorating the Church of Saint Charles, Rubens undertook several great series of paintings, mostly intended for the courts of Europe.

The life of Mary de Medici for the Luxembourg Palace in Paris.
The ceiling of the banqueting hall at Whitehall in London, the hunting lodge of Philip IV near Madrid.

But he was not only a decorator, he was also a brilliant portraitist, and most of the famous and powerful Antwerp citizens of the era wanted one of his paintings. As a result we have splendid portraits of merchants, magistrates, members of the High Clergy, archdukes and foreign princes.
In addition, throughout his life he constantly recorded his own features and those of his family - portraits of his wives Isabella and Helen, of his children, of friends and of himself.

**The commission for
the Descent from the Cross**

On September 7, 1611, the Guild of Gunsmiths, the oldest of the Antwerp guilds and presided over by Nicholas Rockox, Mayor of Antwerp (« buitenburgemesster »), commissioned from Rubens a reredos for the Gunsmiths' Chapel in the Church of Our Lady.

The old guild altar did not blend with the church's more recent furniture and the guild decided to instal a new one. To cover the expense they obtained exemption from military service for those members who were to finance its construction.

The guild wanted a central representation of its patron saint, Christopher, but Rubens tried to respect the decrees of the Council of Thirty, which had been ratified by the provincial council and the diocesan synod in May 1610. According to the decrees, central panels of altar-screens could only feature the figure of Christ or New Testament themes.

Saint Christopher was relegated to the reverse of one of the side panels, though he can be seen when the reredos is closed, its normal position.

When he began work on the reredos Rubens was at the height of his fame and commissions abounded. He had worked in particular on the *Assumption*, which now adorns the master-altar, and the triptych of the *Resurrection* which is in the same church, adorning the grave of Jan Moretus, Plantin's principal collaborator, who died in 1610.

The central panel of the triptych, started some time after September 7, 1611, was completed in September 1612. The side panels were completed with the aid of one or several collaborators in 1614, and were transferred to the cathedral on February 18 and March 16. The triptych was inaugurated by the Bishop of Antwerp on August 24, 1614.

On January 8, 1615, Rubens received an initial payment of 1,000 florins and his wife Isabella was given a pair of gloves. A further sum of 400 Flemish pounds, 1,400 florins, was paid in February 1621.

The iconography of the triptych

The carrying of Christ is the central theme of the triptych. The Virgin Mary carries Jesus before His birth, at the Visitation, Simeon carries the child at the Presentation, the friends of Christ carry Him as they take Him down from the cross, and Saint Christopher carries Christ on his shoulders. On the central panel is the *Descent from the Cross*. A group of people, gathered together in a last gesture of devotion, forms a circle of tenderness and affection around the mortal remains of the Son of God.

In the centre is Christ, eyes glazed, skin bruised and blue, motionless body in a dazzling white shroud which runs right across the picture. The agony is all-consuming. Here is « one of the most tragic figures ever imagined by Rubens to represent God » (Eugene Fromentin).

In a bowl at the foot of the ladder are the crown of thorns and the nails, and beside them the inscription of Pilate and the vinager-soaked sponge which Christ refused.

Saint John supports the body in his arms, and beside him Nicodemus slips his own right arm beneath the body. A man leaning over the bar of the cross and Joseph of Arimathea hold the shroud, and the latter will make his own tomb available for the Saviour. « The Virgin holds back her tears : no cries, no gesticulation, no excessive weeping. She hardly expresses her sorrow with the gestures of an inconsolable mother » (Fromentin).

Following a trend very popular in the Baroque era, great, clearly-defined diagonals cross the whole panel. All the light, the gestures and the figures converge at the centre, the body of Christ.

The colours of the faces are remarkably subtle - the pallor of Christ and Mary, the suntanned helpers, the soft, clear skin of Mary Magdalen. The colours of the clothes harmonise beautifully. The red habit sets off the white of the shroud and the pale body of Christ. On the other side of the painting are the blue-green of Mary, the purple of Mary Cleophas and the olive green of Mary Magdalen. All around the figures darkness stretches away into a tragic sky streaked with barely visible clouds.

The balance between form and expression is perfect. It is a masterly interpretation in which it is all too easy to forget that it was achieved with an artist's brush.

The dimensions of the work are impressive
Height : 4.2 m.
Width of side panels : 1.495 m.
Width of central panel : 3.1 m

The left-hand panel represents the *Visitation* as described by Luke (I, 39-56). Mary and Joseph are being welcomed by Elizabeth and Zacharias on the steps of their house, a rich dwelling evoking the Italian palaces of the Renaissance. Mary is still wearing the hat and sandals she has worn on her journey, and because she is tired she supports herself on the balustrade. Her cousin, who has come out to greet her, points to where she is carrying the future Saviour. Behind Mary an alert young servant carries a basket on his head, containing no doubt the food for the meal.

The Bonnat Museum in Bayonne has a series of preliminary sketches for the *Visitation* which allow an instructive comparison of the various conceptions of the meeting of Mary and Elizabeth to be made. The latter first appears in the doorway, one hand resting on the doorframe. On another she walks down the steps to greet her cousin, and on another she is curtseying. On the final sketch the two women greet each other face to face.

A study in oils at the Museum of Strasbourg suggests the influence of the Veronese *Visitation*, currently in the Barber Institute of Birmingham University. Rubens no doubt borrowed the motif of the balustrade from this work.

Beyond them the surrounding countryside under a blue, cloud-scattered sky can be seen. A peasant goes about his work, a small dog barks at approaching visitors, a peacock struts proudly, a cock and hen peck undisturbed.

On the right-hand panel Rubens painted the *Presentation at the Temple* (Luke II, 22-39). It is a sumptuous temple with subtle tricks of light and depth, with columns, Corinthian pilasters and arches which Rubens must have seen many times during his stay in Italy. The Virgin Mary, in a blue cloak, has presented the child to Simeon who, eyes raised, thanks the heavens. Anne, in the sombre clothes of a widow, smiles at the Infant, and Joseph kneels beside Mary and offers the two ritual doves. Just behind Simeon, among the witnesses, Rubens painted his friend Nicholas Rockox, the Mecaenas who commissioned the reredos and whose portrait he painted more than once.

The composition of the side panels differs very clearly from that of the central panel. Firstly in the conception of space - relief and depth are more accentuated, there is greater use of perspective and the presentation is more anecdotal.
Then in the colours, which are more varied and clearer. In the tricks of light and shade on the faces, the browns of the architecture and blue of the sky Leo van Puyvelde saw an intensifying of the influence of Flemish tradition.
But there is more. The examination carried out by Albert and Paul Philippot at the Institute for Artistic Heritage in Brussels revealed that there had been a collaborator on the side panels. It can be seen by comparing the heads of Joseph in the *Presentation at the Temple* and Nicodemus in the *Descent from the Cross*, both no doubt painted by an assistant whose brushwork was clumsier and much more obvious. Another sign is that the assistant, who lacked his master's technical expertise, used too much pliancy, causing cracks which can be seen, for example, in the heads of Elizabeth and Zacharias in the *Visitation*.

The reverse of the side panels together comprise a single scene dedicated to Saint Christopher, patron saint of gunsmiths. He is a kind of Hercules with an imposing build and powerful muscles. He crosses the ford on a moonlit night, leaning on his staff and carrying Christ on his broad shoulders. The hermit who guides him symbolically casts the light of his lantern on the Infant, the Light of the World.

To create the nocturnal effect the painter chose the darkest of yellows and browns. Above the guide a crescent moon is shining, from one corner an owl watches the whole scene, while down to the right, on the rock where the guide is standing, small lizards play.

The Antwerp master's Saint Christopher seems to have been inspired by the *Farnese Hercules* which he sketched in Rome during his stay in Italy. The model for the saint, in oils on wood and conserved in the Munich Picture Gallery, confirms that the original conception for all three parts of the triptych was Rubens's.

The Rubens technique   Thanks to radiography and micrography we have been able to study the technique of Rubens, the way in which he used and applied his materials.

For the base he used a mixture of animal paste impregnated by a drying oil and chalk. When exposed to the damp this paste peeled off, which explains the scales on the head of Mary Cleophas.

The next coat consisted of a mixture of bone black, white lead and water. This greyish compound darkened the overall preparatory surface.

Rubens then drew with a pigment of bone black, still visible on the coat of the Virgin Mary on the righthand panel.

He mixed his colours with a siccative oil, and to obtain a certain tint he mixed various colours together instead, as the Flemish primitives did, of starting from a clear base and adding layer upon layer until the right colour was found. To the white lead he added malachite (for Mary Magdalen), ochre from the madder root (for Mary Cleophas), vermillion from the madder root (for John the Evangelist) and indigo of lapis-lazuli (for the Virgin Mary on the right-hand panel).

The material used for the triptych

Seventeen oak planks each more than three metres in length were needed for the central panel. They were set horizontally, glued, then joined together by gudgeons and joints. Some of them are visible to the naked eye, for example the one which passes horizontally above the head of Nicodemus and across the left shoulder of Christ.

The side panels consisted of six vertical planks surmounted by six horizontal planks. They were carefully smoothed since they were to be painted on both sides. On the reverse side a coat of black vegetal tar protected them from the damp. They were supported on two large poles, connected by metal stirrups fixed by screws and angle-blocks both stuck to the tar and screwed into the wood.

Four carpenters and two gilders made the protective frames in 1816, according to the inscription on the medallion in the bottom left-hand corner. For the central frame they used spruce, for the side panels pine and lime.

Rubens modified his original conception during his work on the triptych. He removed the forearm and left hand of Mary Cleophas and extended the flow of the shroud. On the right-hand panel he modified the position of the left hand, which was initially much higher.

**Conservation
of the triptych**

In 1728 the Guild Council decided that the constant opening
and closing of the panels was likely to damage the painting.
They therefore had the side panels sawn in two and the face
on which Saint Christopher appeared was taken to the
Gunsmiths' House and replaced by a copy.

On August 5, 1794, the occupying French had the triptych
sent to the Saint Michel Abbey, and from there the central
panel was taken by boat to Lille and then by road to Paris. It
was exhibited at the Louvre from September 23, 1794.

The triptych left the Napoleon Museum on October 31, 1815,
following the Battle of Waterloo, and on November 27 it
reached Brussels. Before the end of the year it was back in
Antwerp and on May 31, 1816, it was re-installed in the
cathedral.

Fine Arts Museum, and from 1940 to 1946 it was hidden
beneath the south tower of the cathedral.

The triptych has been restored about ten times, most notably
in 1728, 1754-56, 1773, 1816 and 1898. On July 7, 1960, it
was taken to the Royal Institute for Artistic Heritage in
Brussels for a thorough restoration. A team of specialists
studied it, treated it and generally prepared it for its long
future life.

**Rubens,
artist and craftsman**

Silhouettes and outlines clearly drawn, the predominance of certain splashes of colour such as white or bright red, light shining obliquely, silver and golden and sometimes with the effect of enamel - "the Rubens effect," as Delacroix was to remark.

Voluptuous, consuming, full of life and whirling movement, a feast for the eye. "Life flows endlessly here, like the air in the sky, like the water in the sea" (Charles Baudelaire).

This is one of Rubens's most masterly works, a high point of pictorial creation which could not fail to have an influence on the great painters of the West. But we should not be misled. This painting, like all of Rubens's canvases, is the result of patient, systematic and efficient research.

First came an outline of the
principal subject, swift and almost
always in monochrome. Then some
more precise sketches and
experiments with colour, and
finally the picture itself. Assistants
prepared the panel and the
canvases, mixed the colours, got
the various brushes ready.
Sometimes followers of the master
like Van Dijck or Snyders helped
him.

LVCAS VORSTERMANS

Desine Lysippos iac̄are animosa vetus Pas
Hic Vir, hic excudit spirantia mollius æra.

Ant. van Dyck pinxit   *Luc Vorstermans iunior sculpsit et excudit*

Often pupils copied the works while engravers like Lucas
Vorsterman reproduced them and sent them around the
world.
A far cry from the apparently spontaneous natural
expression, the inspiration which is immediately put down on
canvas. But Rubens was as much a craftsman as a genius.

The *Descent from the Cross*
is a dazzling example
of the combination of the artist's craft
and impulsive inspiration,
a harnessing of creative enthusiasm
by complete control of all the skills.

Bibliography

Liège

Collon-Gevaert S., *Histoire des arts du métal en Belgique*, Académie Royale de Belgique, Classe des Beaux-Arts, Mémoires, 2nd séries, t. VII, Brussels, 1951, pp. 133-148.

Collon-Gevaert S., Lejeune J. and Stiennon J., *Art roman dans la vallée de la Meuse aux XIe et XIIe siècles*, Brussels, 1962.

Gevaert S., *Le problème des représentations figurées dans les fonts baptismaux de Renier de Huy (1107-1118)*, in « Revue belge d'Archéologie et d'Histoire de l'Art », t. XII, 1942, pp. 169-182.

Laurent M., *La question des fonts de Saint-Barthélemy de Liège*, in « Bulletin monumental », t. LXXXIII, 1924, pp. 327-348.

Legner A., *Die Rinderherde des Renier von Huy*, in « Rhein und Maas. Kunst und Kultur 800-1400 », t. II, pp. 237-250.

Lejeune J. *A propos de l'art mosan... Renier l'orfèvre, et les fonts de Notre-Dame*, in « Anciens Pays et Assemblées d'Etats », t. III, 1952.

Puraye J., Evrard E. and Curvers A., *Essais sur les Fonts baptismaux de l'église Saint-Barthélemy à Liège*, in « La Vie Wallonne », t. XXVI, 1952, pp. 157-197.

Stiennon J., *L'art roman. Un âge d'or*, in « La Wallonie. Le Pays et les Hommes », t. I, Bruxelles, 1977, pp. 231-250.

Usener K. H., *Reiner von Huy und seine künstlerische Nachfolge*, in « Marburger Jahrbuch für Kunstwissenschaft », t. VII, 1933.

Tournai

Cassart J., *La restauration de la châsse de Notre-Dame en 1889-1890*, in « Annales de la Société Royale d'Histoire et d'Archéologie de Tournai », pp. 96-110.

Cloquet J., *La châsse de Notre-Dame de Tournai*, in « Bulletin de la Société historique et littéraire de Tournai », n° 24 (1894), pp. 406-432.

Demus O., *Zu Niklaus von Verdun*, in « Intuition und Kunstwissenschaft. Festschrift für H. Swarzenski », Berlin, 1973.

Warichez J., *La cathédrale de Tournai et son chapitre*, Wetteren, 1934.

Exhibition catalogs

Der Meister der Dreiköningen-Schreins. Exhibition, Cologne, 1964.

The Year 1200. A Centennial Exhibition, New York, 1970.

Rhin-Meuse, Cologne-Brussels, 1972.

Namur

Collon-Gevaert S., *Histoire des arts du métal en Belgique*, Brussels, 1951.

Collon-Gevaert S., Lejeune J., Stiennon J., *L'art mosan aux XIe et XIIe siècles*, Bruxelles, 1951.

Courtoy F., *Le trésor du prieuré d'Oignies aux Sœurs de Notre-Dame à Namur et l'œuvre du frère Hugo*, in « Bulletin de la Commission royale des Monuments et des Sites », Brussels, 1951-1952.

Link E.M., *Hugo von Oignies*, Fribourg-en-Brisgau, 1964.

Poncelet E., *Chartes du prieuré d'Oignies*, in « Annales de la Société archéologique de Namur », t. 31, Namur, 1913.

Stiennon J., *Art mosan aux XIe et XIIe siècles*, Brussels, 1962.

Toussaint, *Histoire du monastère d'Oignies*, Namur, 1880.

Exhibition catalogs

Malines (1864), Brussels (1880 et 1888), Bruges (1902), Liège (1905), Charleroi (1911), Paris (1924), Namur (1930), Liège (1951), Paris (1968), Cologne/Brussels (1972).

Ghent

Coremans P. et Janssens de Bisthoven A., *Van Eyck, L'Adoration de l'Agneau mystique*, Antwerp-Amsterdam, 1948, pp. 39-42.

Dhanens E., *Van Eyck. The Ghent Altarpiece. Art in Context*, London-New York, Allen Lane-Viking Press, 1973.

Duverger J., *De Navorsing betreffende de Van Eyck's*, in « Het Oude Land van Loon », t. IX (1954), pp. 192-210.

Friedländer M. J., (*Die Altniederländische Malerei), Early Netherlandish Painting*, Brussels-Leiden, 1967, Editor's Note, pp. 105-106, t. XIV, Supplemènts, pp. 1-4.

Fris V., *Bibliographie des Van Eyck*, in Bulletin de la Société d'Histoire et d'Archéologie de Gand », t. XIV (1906), pp. 313-333.

James-Weale W. H., *Hubert and John Van Eyck, their life and work*, London-New York, 1908, pp. LV-CXIV.

Curvers A., *La Théologie secrète de la prétendue Adoration de l'Agneau*, in « Approches de l'Art », Brussels, 1973.

Bruges

Eemans M., *Hans Memling*, Brussels, 1970.

Faggin G.T. et Corti M., *Tout l'œuvre peint de Memling*, Paris, 1973.

Farlane K. B. Mc, *Hans Memling*, Oxford, 1971.

Friedländer M.J., *Memling*, Amsterdam, 1949.

Friedländer M.J., *Early Netherlandish Painting*, vol VI, « Hans Memling and Gerard David », Brussels-Leiden, 1971.

Guillaume-Linephty M., *Hans Memling à l'hôpital*

Saint-Jean de Bruges, Paris-Brussels, 1939.
Guillame-Linephty M., *La châsse de sainte Ursule*, Brussels, 1958.
Lambotte P., *Hans Memling, le maître de la châsse de sainte Ursule*, Antwerp, 1939.
Lavalleye J., *Hans Memling*, Bruges, 1939.
Lavalleye J., *Memling à l'hôpital Saint-Jean*, Brussels, 1953.
Marlier G., *Memling*, Brussels, 1934.
Penninck J., *Het Sint-Janhospitaal en het Memlingmuseum*, Bruges, 1973.
von Baldass L., *Hans Memling*, Vienne, 1942.
Weale W. H. J., *Hans Memlinc,* Bruges, 1871.
Weale W. H. J., *Hans Memlinc*, Bruges, 1901.

Exhibition catalogs
Memling, Bruges 1939.
De eeuw der Vlaamse Primitieven, Bruges 1960.
Sint-Janhospitaal Brugge. 1188-1976, 2 vol., Bruges, 1976.

Brussels

On the painting :
Roberts-Jones Ph., *La Chute d'Icare*, Office du Livre, Fribourg, 1974.
Collection : *Les Chefs-d'œuvre absolus de la peinture*, edited by Jean Guichard-Meili.

On Peter Brueghel :
Arpino G. and Bianconi P., *L'opera completa di Bruegel*, Milan, 1967.
Claessens B. et Rousseau J., *Notre Bruegel*, Antwerp, 1969.
Delevoy R.L., *Bruegel,* Geneva, 1959.
de Tolnay Ch., *Pierre Bruegel l'Ancien*, Brussels, 1935.
Friedländer M.J., *Pieter Bruegel*, in « Die Altniederländische Malerei », t. XVI, Leiden, 1937.
Fierens P., *Peter Bruegel, sa vie, son œuvre, son temps*, Paris, 1949.
Genaille R., *Bruegel l'Ancien*, Paris, 1953.
Glück G., *Das grosse Bruegel-Werk*, Vienna, 1953.
Grossman F., *Bruegel, The Paintings*, London, 1955.
Lavalleye J., *Lucas van Leyden. Peter Bruegel l'Ancien. Gravures*, Paris, 1966.
Marijnissen R. H., *Bruegel le Vieux*, Brussels, 1969.
Menzel G. W., *Pieter Bruegel der Altere*, Leipzig, 1966.
Van Puyvelde, L., *La peinture au siècle de Bosch et de Bruegel*, Paris, 1962.

Antwerp

Avermaete R., *Rubens et son temps*, Antwerp, 1977.
Baudouin F., *Pierre-Paul Rubens*, Antwerp, 1977.

Burchard L. and d'Hulst R. A., *Rubens Drawings*, 2 vols., Brussels, 1963.

Cabanne P., *Rubens*, Paris, 1966.

Corpus Rubenianum Ludwig Burchard.

Jaffe M., *Un chef-d'œuvre mieux connu*, in « L'Œil », n° 43/44, 1958.

Martin J.R., *The Antwerp Altarpieces*, New York, 1969.

Odenbourg R., *Peter-Paul Rubens*, Munich-Berlin, 1922.

Rooses M., *L'œuvre de Pierre-Paul Rubens. Histoire et description de ses tableaux et dessins*, 5 vol., Antwerp, 1886-1892.

Van Brabant J., *Onze-Lieve-Vrouw Kathedraal van Antwerpen*, Antwerp, 1972.

Van Puyvelde L., *Rubens*, (new edition) Brussels, 1977.

Sources of illustrations

Contents